AMERICAN EMPOWER

STUDENT'S BOOK A
WITH DIGITAL PACK

T0349643

B2

UPPER INTERMEDIATE

Adrian Doff, Craig Thaine
Herbert Puchta, Jeff Stranks, Peter Lewis-Jones

AMERICAN EMPOWER

AMERICAN EMPOWER is a six-level general English course for adult and young adult learners, taking students from beginner to advanced level (CEFR A1 to C1). *American Empower* combines course content from Cambridge University Press with validated assessment from the experts at Cambridge Assessment English.

American Empower's unique mix of engaging classroom materials and reliable assessment enables learners to make consistent and measurable progress.

Content you'll love.

Assessment you can trust.

> **7.4 Writing task:...** 🔔 👤 Carlos ∨
>
> **Writing task: An opinion on future food**
>
> What food will people eat in the future? Do you think people will eat insects or meat made by scientists? Write your opinion.
>
> Use *I (don't) think, If you ask me,* and *For me.*
>
> Answer:
>
> Type here ...

CAN DO OBJECTIVES
- Discuss possible future events
- Prepare for a job interview
- Discuss advantages and disadvantages
- Write an argument for and against an idea

CHANCE

UNIT **5**

GETTING STARTED

a 🗨 Look at the picture and answer the questions.
1 What is the woman doing?
2 Would you like to try something like that? Why / Why not?
3 What could the woman be thinking?
4 Imagine you're on the beach below. What would you be thinking?

b 🗨 Discuss the questions.
1 Why do you think some people like doing extreme and dangerous things?
2 Do you think they do these things in spite of the risk or because of the risk?

55

Better Learning with *American Empower*

Better Learning is our simple approach where **insights** we've gained from research have helped shape **content** that drives **results** .

Learner engagement

1 Content that informs and motivates

Insights
Sustained motivation is key to successful language learning and skills development.

Content
Clear learning goals, thought-provoking images, texts, and speaking activities, plus video content to arouse curiosity.

Results
Content that surprises, entertains, and provokes an emotional response, helping teachers to deliver motivating and memorable lessons.

5A YOU COULD LIVE TO BE A HUNDRED

Learn to discuss possible future events
G Future probability
V Adjectives describing attitude

1 SPEAKING

Are you an OPTIMIST or a PESSIMIST?

a ⬚ Are you an optimist or a pessimist? Mark your place on this scale, then compare with others in your group.

Optimist ⬌ Pessimist

b ⬚ Decide what you think about the questions, then compare your answers.

1 If you take a test at the end of this class, how well will you do?

I'll get a perfect score. ⬌ I'll probably fail.

2 Do you expect the coming week to be … ?

exciting/great ⬌ boring/terrible

3 Imagine you left your bag on the bus. Do you expect to get it back?

Yes ⬌ No

4 You start a new workout routine and you're really tired the next day. Do you expect it to be easier the next time?

Yes ⬌ No

c ⬚ Communication 5A Now go to p. 129.

d ⬚ Based on your answers in 1b, decide who in your group … ?
• is the most optimistic
• is the most pessimistic
• is the most realistic

e Write a question to find out if other students are optimistic or pessimistic. Add a) and b) answer choices.
Example:
You want to buy a shirt you like, but the store is sold out. What do you think?
a) I'm sure I can find it somewhere else.
b) Why am I always so unlucky?

56

WHY WE THINK WE'RE GOING TO HAVE A LONG AND HAPPY LIFE

Researchers have found that people all over the world share an important characteristic: optimism. Sue Reynolds explains what it's all about.

… we keep polluting the planet because we're sure that we'll find a way to clean it up some day …

WE'RE ALL ABOVE AVERAGE!
Try asking a 20-year-old these questions:
• What kind of career will you have?
• How long do you think you'll live?

Most people think they'll be able to earn above-average salaries, but only some of the population can make that much. Most young men in Europe will say they expect to live well into their 80s, but the average life expectancy for European men is 75. Most people don't take out travel insurance because they're sure everything will be all right, they don't worry about saving up for old age because the future looks fine, or they smoke cigarettes in spite of the health warnings on the pack because they believe "It won't happen to me." Or on a global scale, we keep polluting the planet because we're sure that we'll find a way to clean it up some day in the future.

OPTIMISM IS GOOD FOR YOU
But researchers believe that the Optimism Bias is actually good for us. People who expect the best are generally likely to be ambitious and adventurous, whereas people who expect the worst are likely to be more cautious, so optimism actually helps to make us successful. Optimists are also healthier because they feel less stress – they can relax because they think that everything is going to be just fine. Not only that, but the Optimism Bias may also have played an important part in our evolution as human beings. Because we hoped for the best, we were prepared to take risks such as hunting down dangerous animals and traveling across the sea to find new places to live, and this is why we became so successful as a species. Even if our optimism is unrealistic and leads us to take risks, without it we might all still be living in caves, too afraid to go outside and explore the world in case we get eaten by wild animals.

Most people are also optimistic about their own strengths and abilities. Ask people, "How well do you get along with other people?" or "How intelligent are the people in your family?" and they'll usually say they're above average. Again, they can't all be right. We can't all be better than everyone else, but that's what we think.

LOOKING ON THE BRIGHT SIDE
There is a reason for this. Research has shown that, on the whole, we are optimistic by nature and have a positive view of ourselves. In fact, we are much more optimistic than realistic and frequently imagine things will turn out better than they actually do. Most people don't expect their marriages to end in divorce, they don't expect to lose their jobs, or to be diagnosed with a life-threatening disease. Furthermore, when things do go wrong, they are often quick to find something positive in all the gloom. Many people who fail exams, for example, are convinced they were just unlucky with the questions and they'll do better next time. Or people who have had a serious illness often say that it was really positive because it made them appreciate life more. We really are very good at "looking on the bright side."

THE OPTIMISM BIAS
This certainty that our future is bound to be better than our past and present is known as the "Optimism Bias," and researchers have found that it is common to people all over the world and of all ages. Of course, the Optimism Bias can lead us to make some very bad decisions. Often, people don't take out travel insurance because they're

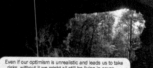
Even if our optimism is unrealistic and leads us to take risks, without it we might all still be living in caves …

UNIT 5

2 READING

a Read the article "Why We Think We're Going to Have a Long and Happy Life" quickly. Choose the correct words to complete the summary.
Most people are naturally *optimistic / pessimistic*, and this is generally *an advantage / a disadvantage* for the human race because it helps us to be *realistic about the future / more successful*.

b Read the article again. Check (✓) the five points made in the article.
1 ⬚ Pessimists usually have fewer friends than optimists.
2 ⬚ Humans are naturally positive about their future.
3 ⬚ Reality is often worse than we imagine it to be.
4 ⬚ People who live in warmer countries are usually more optimistic.
5 ⬚ We often act (or don't act) because we're confident everything will work out.
6 ⬚ If we imagine a better future, we will take more risks.
7 ⬚ Optimists spend a lot of time daydreaming.
8 ⬚ Optimism about the future makes us feel better in the present.

c Discuss the questions.
• Look again at your answers in 1b. Do you think you have the "Optimism Bias"?
• Do you agree that it's better to be optimistic than realistic? Why / Why not?
• How do you see yourself 20 years from now?

3 VOCABULARY
Adjectives describing attitude

a Find adjectives in "Why We Think We're Going to Have a Long and Happy Life" that mean:
1 expecting the future to be good
2 seeing things as they are
3 not seeing things as they are
4 prepared to take risks
5 not prepared to take risks
6 wanting to be successful

b Which of these adjectives best describe you?

c ⬚ Now go to Vocabulary Focus 5A on p. 158.

Many people who fail exams are convinced they were just unlucky with the questions …

57

---

2 Personalized and relevant

Insights
Language learners benefit from frequent opportunities to personalize their responses.

Content
Personalization tasks in every unit make the target language more meaningful to the individual learner.

Results
Personal responses make learning more memorable and inclusive, with all students participating in spontaneous spoken interaction.

> ❝ There are so many adjectives to describe such a wonderful series, but in my opinion it's very reliable, practical, and modern. ❞
>
> **Zenaide Brianez, Director of Studies, Instituto da Língua Inglesa, Brazil**

Measurable progress

1 Assessment you can trust

Insights
Tests developed and validated by Cambridge Assessment English, the world leaders in language assessment, to ensure they are accurate and meaningful.

Content
End-of-unit tests, mid- and end-of-course competency tests, and personalized CEFR test report forms provide reliable information on progress with language skills.

Results
Teachers can see learners' progress at a glance, and learners can see measurable progress, which leads to greater motivation.

Results of an impact study showing % improvement of Reading levels, based on global *Empower* students' scores over one year.

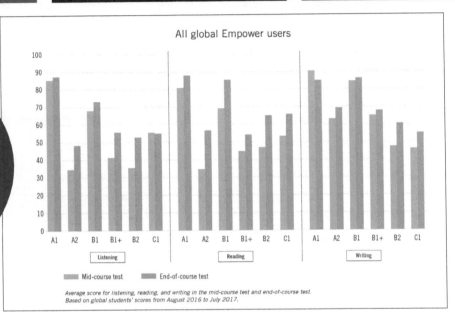

All global Empower users

Average score for listening, reading, and writing in the mid-course test and end-of-course test.
Based on global students' scores from August 2016 to July 2017.

Mid-course test End-of-course test

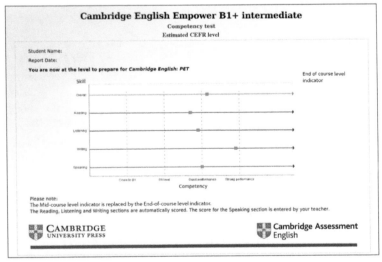

Cambridge English Empower B1+ intermediate
Competency test
Estimated CEFR level

Student Name:
Report Date:
You are now at the level to prepare for *Cambridge English: PET*

Please note:
The Mid-course level indicator is replaced by the End-of-course level indicator.
The Reading, Listening and Writing sections are automatically scored. The score for the Speaking section is entered by your teacher.

CAMBRIDGE UNIVERSITY PRESS   Cambridge Assessment English

> "We started using the tests provided with Empower and our students started showing better results from this point until now."

Kristina Ivanova, Director of Foreign Language Training Centre, ITMO University, Saint Petersburg, Russia

2 Evidence of impact

Insights
Schools and colleges need to show that they are evaluating the effectiveness of their language programs.

Content
Empower (British English) impact studies have been carried out in various countries, including Russia, Brazil, Turkey, and the UK, to provide evidence of positive impact and progress.

Results
Colleges and universities have demonstrated a significant improvement in language level between the mid- and end-of-course tests, as well as a high level of teacher satisfaction with *Empower*.

Manageable learning

1 Mobile friendly

Insights
Learners expect online content to be mobile friendly but also flexible and easy to use on any digital device.

Content
American Empower provides easy access to Digital Workbook content that works on any device and includes practice activities with audio.

Results
Digital Workbook content is easy to access anywhere, and produces meaningful and actionable data so teachers can track their students' progress and adapt their lesson accordingly.

"I had been studying English for 10 years before university, and I didn't succeed. But now with Empower *I know my level of English has changed.*"

Nikita, *Empower* Student, ITMO University, Saint Petersburg, Russia

2 Corpus-informed

Insights
Corpora can provide valuable information about the language items learners are able to learn successfully at each CEFR level.

Content
Two powerful resources – Cambridge Corpus and English Profile – informed the development of the *Empower* course syllabus and the writing of the materials.

Results
Learners are presented with the target language they are able to incorporate and use at the right point in their learning journey. They are not overwhelmed with unrealistic learning expectations.

Rich in practice

1 Language in use

Insights
It is essential that learners are offered frequent and manageable opportunities to practice the language they have been focusing on.

Content
Throughout the *American Empower* Student's Book, learners are offered a wide variety of practice activities, plenty of controlled practice, and frequent opportunities for communicative spoken practice.

Results
Meaningful practice makes new language more memorable and leads to more efficient progress in language acquisition.

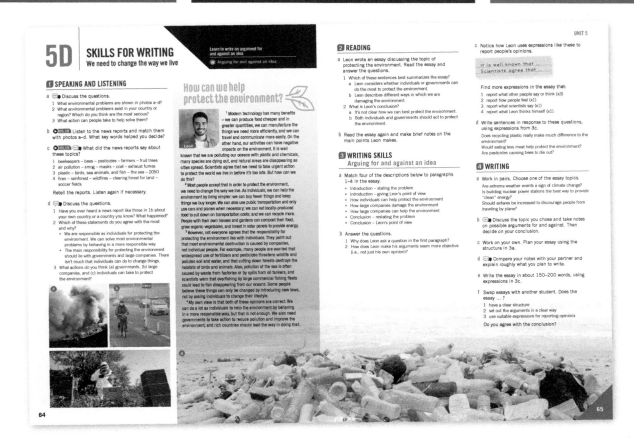

2 Beyond the classroom

> *There are plenty of opportunities for personalization.*
>
> **Elena Pro, Teacher, EOI de San Fernando de Henares, Spain**

Insights
Progress with language learning often requires work outside of the classroom, and different teaching models require different approaches.

Content
American Empower is available with a print workbook, online practice, documentary-style videos that expose learners to real-world English, plus additional resources with extra ideas and fun activities.

Results
This choice of additional resources helps teachers to find the most effective ways to motivate their students both inside and outside the classroom.

Unit overview

Unit Opener

Getting started page – Clear learning objectives to give an immediate sense of purpose.

↓

Lessons A and B

Grammar and Vocabulary – Input and practice of core grammar and vocabulary, plus a mix of skills.

— Digital Workbook (online, mobile): Grammar and Vocabulary

↓

Lesson C

Everyday English – Functional language in common, everyday situations.

— Digital Workbook (online, mobile): Listening and Speaking

↓

Unit Progress Test

↓

Lesson D

Integrated Skills – Practice of all four skills, with a special emphasis on writing.

— Digital Workbook (online, mobile): Reading and Writing

↓

Review

Extra practice of grammar, vocabulary, and pronunciation. Also a "Review your progress" section for students to reflect on the unit.

↓

Mid- / End-of-course test

↓

Additional practice

Further practice is available for outside of the class with these components.

Digital Workbook (online, mobile)

Workbook (printed)

Components

Resources – Available on cambridgeone.org

- Audio
- Video
- Unit Progress Tests (Print)
- Unit Progress Tests (Online)

- Mid- and end-of-course assessment (Print)
- Mid- and end-of-course assessment (Online)

- Digital Workbook (Online)
- Photocopiable Grammar, Vocabulary, and Pronunciation worksheets

CONTENTS

This page is intentionally left blank.

This page is intentionally left blank.

This page is intentionally left blank.

⟲ CAN DO OBJECTIVES

- Discuss people you admire
- Discuss a challenge
- Explain what to do and check understanding
- Write an article

UNIT **1**

OUTSTANDING PEOPLE

GETTING STARTED

a 💬🔊 Look at the picture and answer the questions.

1 Who do you think the people taking a selfie are? Where are they?
2 What are the people around them doing?
3 What do you think they have just said to each other? What's going to happen next?

b 💬🔊 Discuss the questions.

1 On what occasions do you normally take photos?
2 If you could take a selfie with a famous person, who would you choose and why?
3 What role do you think famous people play in society? Should they be good role models? Should they inspire other people?

1 READING

a 💬 What kinds of people do you admire most? Why?

b 💬 Look at photos a and b. What do you think these people have done to make other people admire them?

c Read "Apple's Design Genius" and "The Woman Who Reinvented Children's TV" quickly and check your answers.

d Read the texts again and answer the questions. Write *JI* (Jony Ive), *JGC* (Joan Ganz Cooney), or *B* (both).

Who … ?
1 had training in their area of work
2 carried out some research
3 set up their own company
4 was one of the first people in their role
5 initially found the work challenging
6 was interested in other people's learning
7 believes the things we use should be beautiful
8 has won prizes for their work

e 💬 Who do you think is more inspiring, Jony Ive or Joan Ganz Cooney? Why?

Apple's Design Genius

I've always loved great design. Ever since I can remember, I've been fascinated by the shape and look of objects. In my opinion, Apple Inc. is the number one company in the world for product design.

In the time that [1]**you're reading** this article, around 750 iPhones and 300 iPads will be sold internationally. These iconic devices generate millions of dollars a day for Apple, and the man behind their iconic look is known as a "design genius." *Time* magazine once listed him as one of the 100 most influential people in the world, but can you name him?

If you said Steve Jobs, you'd be wrong, although it was Jobs who first recognized this man's talent. His name is Jony Ive.

Born in London, Jony Ive studied industrial design in college. After graduating, [2]**he helped** set up the London design agency Tangerine. In 1992, while [3]**he was working** at Tangerine, he accepted a job offer from Apple.

His first years in the job were tough, and the design work wasn't very interesting. The company was also struggling to make money. However, when Steve Jobs returned to Apple in 1997 and saw the design work that Ive [4]**had produced**, he immediately recognized Ive's ability and promoted him. Ive's first success in his new role was the design of the original, colorful iMac in 1998, which was quickly followed by the first iPod in 2001. Thanks to Ive's simple, elegant designs, Apple became one of the most successful companies in the world. From then, until his retirement in 2019, he was responsible for the iPhone, iPad, and Apple Watch. Ive's designs involved not only the way these products look but also the way they work. [5]**He believes** devices have to be both beautiful and practical.

Jony Ive's key contribution to Apple is recognized, and [6]**he has received** numerous awards for his designs. There is no doubt that Steve Jobs was a larger-than-life idea man and businessperson who created a hugely successful company. However, without Jony Ive's design talent, Apple may not have become such a huge success.

So what have I learned from Jony Ive? That the best designs are often the simplest.

THE WOMAN WHO REINVENTED CHILDREN'S TV

I've always felt passionate about television's ability to entertain and educate. I grew up watching what I consider to be a master class in how you can combine these two aspects of television: *Sesame Street*. This is the show that brought us Big Bird, Elmo, Cookie Monster, and more. These characters were brought to TV thanks to a woman I consider a genius: Joan Ganz Cooney.

In the mid-1960s, Ganz Cooney was working as a producer of television documentary shows in America. She realized television could play an important role in the education of preschool children. She researched this idea and, in 1967, she wrote an outline for *Sesame Street*.

Ganz Cooney presented her ideas to the TV network she was working for at the time. However, the network rejected her proposal, saying that they thought she didn't have the right experience to produce a TV show for children. As a result, she set up Children's Television Workshop with a colleague, and two years later they had managed to raise $8 million to finance production. Even so, many people working in the television industry questioned her ability to manage such a project. This was during the 1960s, when the industry was largely controlled by men.

At first, Ganz Cooney didn't want to fight to keep her role as the director of the production company and the producer of the show. However, her husband and a colleague encouraged her to do so because they knew the project would fail without her involvement. This meant she became one of the first female television executives in the United States.

In 1969, two years after her initial research, *Sesame Street* went on the air, and today it's still going strong. However, Joan Ganz Cooney didn't stop there. She continued to take an interest in early childhood education, and in 2007, the Joan Ganz Cooney Center was founded to help improve children's digital literacy. I really admire the way she continued helping young children. She's not a household name like Big Bird, but she's won many awards for her work and had a huge impact on the education of millions of children around the world.

Sesame Street Facts
- more than 150 million viewers worldwide
- shown in more than 150 different countries
- now has a production budget of around $17 million a year

2 GRAMMAR Review of tenses

a Match the verbs 1–6 in **bold** in "Apple's Design Genius" with the tenses below.

- ☐ simple present
- ☐ simple past
- ☐ present continuous
- ☐ past continuous
- ☐ present perfect
- ☐ past perfect

b Complete the sentences with the tenses in 2a.
We use the:
1 _____ to refer to an event that takes place at a specific time in the past.
2 _____ to refer to a temporary event in progress in the present.
3 _____ to refer to a state or action that began in the past and has continued until now.
4 _____ to refer to something that's generally true.
5 _____ to refer to an action that was in progress in the past when something else happened.
6 _____ to refer to a past action that occurred before another past action.

c <u>Underline</u> examples of the six tenses in the second text.

d ≫ Now go to Grammar Focus 1A on p. 134.

e Read the text about Nikola Tesla and underline the correct words.

f ▶ 01.02 Listen and check your answers.

NIKOLA TESLA 〜

Not many people [1]*have heard / heard* of Nikola Tesla, who [2]*played / was playing* a key role in creating the alternating current (AC) supply of electricity we [3]*are having / have* in our homes today. Early in his career, Tesla [4]*has worked / worked* with Thomas Edison. He [5]*had emigrated / has emigrated* to the U.S. from Europe in 1884. While Tesla [6]*was working / had worked* for Edison, they had an argument over payment for an invention, so Tesla [7]*was deciding / decided* to work independently. It was then that he developed a motor that could produce an alternating current. Throughout his life, Tesla continued to conduct experiments and [8]*helped / was helping* develop X-ray radiography and wireless communication. There is no doubt that he [9]*has had / had had* a large impact on modern technology. Many of the gadgets that we [10]*are enjoying / enjoy* today would not have been possible without Nikola Tesla.

3 LISTENING

a ▶ 01.03 Listen to two roommates, Amelia and Chloe, talking about a female scientist, Jocelyn Bell-Burnell. Check (✓) the correct sentences.

1 She's always been famous. ☐
2 She isn't very well known. ☐
3 She made an amazing discovery. ☐
4 She created a new mathematical theory. ☐

b ▶ 01.03 Listen again. Are the sentences true or false?

1 Amelia's reading a nonfiction book about planets and stars.
2 Jocelyn Bell-Burnell discovered a kind of star.
3 Bell-Burnell won a Nobel Prize for her discovery.
4 Bell-Burnell did badly when studying science in high school.
5 Life wasn't easy for her when she made her discovery.
6 The press didn't treat Bell-Burnell seriously.
7 Amelia has been inspired by Jocelyn Bell-Burnell.

c 💬🗩 Discuss the questions.

1 Could Jocelyn Bell-Burnell's story have happened in your country? Do you know any similar examples?
2 How popular is science in your country? Is it popular with both men and women?
3 Is it important what gender a scientist is? Why do you think it was important in the case of Jocelyn Bell-Burnell?

4 VOCABULARY
Character adjectives

a Underline the five adjectives that describe people's character in sentences 1–4. Which two adjectives have a similar meaning, and what's the difference between them?

1 She's a respected physicist.
2 She is an inspiring woman.
3 She was really determined, but in a quiet way.
4 Well, you've always been motivated, that's for sure. And stubborn.

b ▶ 01.04 **Pronunciation** Listen to the pronunciation of the letter *e* in these words. Which two sounds are the same? What are the other two sounds?

re<u>s</u>p<u>e</u>cted   d<u>e</u>t<u>e</u>rmined

c ▶ 01.05 Look at the words in the box and decide how the <u>underlined</u> letter *e* is pronounced. Add the words to the chart, then listen and check. Practice saying the words.

| slept   r<u>e</u>vise   h<u>e</u>lpful   s<u>e</u>rve   d<u>e</u>sire |
| pr<u>e</u>fer   id<u>e</u>ntity   univ<u>e</u>rsity   wom<u>e</u>n |

Sound 1 /ɪ/	Sound 2 /e/	Sound 3 /ɜ/

d Complete the sentences with the character adjectives in 4a.

1 Once Dan gets an idea in his head, nothing will change his mind. He's the most _____ person I know, and it's really annoying.
2 I'm not the sort of person who gives up easily – I'm very _____ to achieve new goals.
3 He's worked hard and has done some very interesting research. He's a highly _____ chemist who's known around the world.
4 Doing a PhD is hard work, so you have to be really _____ if you want to complete one.
5 In my last year of high school, we had a really _____ biology teacher. Her lessons were so interesting that we all worked very hard for her.

e ⟫ Now go to Vocabulary Focus on p. 154.

5 SPEAKING

a Think of an inspiring person who has influenced you in some way. It can be someone you know or someone famous. Take notes about the person. Use the questions to help you.

• What is this person's background?
• What important things has this person done in their life?
• Why are they inspiring?
• How have they changed or influenced your life?

b 💬🗩 Tell other students about your person. Ask questions.

How does she stay motivated?

My cousin Vera is an athlete. She trains really hard every day – she's very determined.

1B | ARE YOU FINDING IT DIFFICULT?

Learn to discuss a challenge

G Questions

V Trying and succeeding

1 SPEAKING AND LISTENING

a 💬 Look at photos a–c and read "The 30-Day Challenge." Then discuss the questions.

1 What are the people in the photos doing? Have you ever taken up similar activities? If so, how successful were you?

2 Do you think doing something for 30 days gives you a better chance of succeeding? Why / Why not?

b ▶ 01.09 Listen to a podcast about the 30-day challenge. Check (✓) the main point that Alison makes.

1 The 30-day challenge is the only way to give up bad habits.

2 It's too difficult for the brain to adapt to new habits.

3 If you try something new for 30 days, you're more likely to stick with it afterward.

c ▶ 01.09 Alison took some notes at the seminar. Complete her notes with one or two words in each blank. Listen again and check.

The 30-Day Challenge

Have you ever started a new hobby but given up after only a couple of weeks? Or started a class and stopped after the first few lessons? Most of us have tried to learn something new, but very few of us ever really get any good at it – it's just too difficult to continue doing something new.

But now there's some good news: did you know that if you can keep up your new hobby for just 30 days, you have a much better chance of succeeding? And you may learn something new about yourself, too.

Seminar Notes

- It takes the brain 30 days to adapt to a new ¹_____
- 30 days isn't a ²_____ time, so it's fun to challenge yourself.
- Also a chance to try something ³_____ – not just giving up bad habits.
- Two ways to do it:
  1 do something that doesn't get in the way of your ⁴_____
  2 take time out to do something you've always ⁵_____ do
- You need to make an ⁶_____!

d What examples of 30-day challenges did you hear? Use words from both boxes for each challenge.

Bike everywhere, even in the rain.

~~bike~~	drink	climb	get up	cook	paint	write

sunrise	poem	coffee	meal	picture
mountain	~~rain~~			

e What do you think of the ideas Alison talks about? Take notes.

f 💬 Compare your ideas.

11

2 VOCABULARY
Trying and succeeding

a ▶01.10 Complete the sentences with the phrases in the box. Listen and check your answers.

give up   take a chance   keep it up   stick with
make an effort   manage to   drop out
try out   work out

1 Often if we try something new, we _____ after about a week or two because our brain hasn't adapted.
2 So if you _____ do something new for a month, you'll probably _____ it.
3 Maybe you wouldn't want to _____ for your whole life, but it might be fun to do it just for 30 days.
4 If you're successful it's great, but if it doesn't _____, it doesn't matter too much.
5 It's not just about giving up bad habits. The idea is that you _____ on something new.
6 You can be motivated and _____ something you've always wanted to do.
7 You must _____ to complete your goal.
8 Don't _____ of the challenge! Keep going and you will succeed.

b Match words and phrases from 2a with the meanings.

1 succeed _____, _____
2 stop trying _____, _____
3 not stop trying _____, _____
4 try hard _____
5 try to see if it works _____, _____

c Complete the sentences below about 30-day challenges. Use the words and phrases in 2a and your own ideas. There is more than one possible answer.

1 He tried giving up coffee for 30 days. It wasn't easy, but he …
2 You have woken up at 5:30 every morning for three weeks now. You only have one week to go, so …
3 Thirty-day challenges sound fun. I want to do something different, so I think I'll …

d 💬🗨 Work in small groups. Tell the group about a time when you:

- found something difficult but didn't give up
- made a real effort to succeed
- took a chance at something unusual
- managed to do something that worked out successfully
- tried to do something that didn't work out.

3 READING

a Look at challenges 1–3. Who do you think will find it easy and who will find it difficult?

b Read the interviews and check your ideas.

30-DAY
CHALLENGE

**Challenge 1:
Sofia decided
not to eat meat.**

What made you decide to become a vegetarian, Sofia?

Well, for a long time now I've been trying to eat less meat, partly for health reasons. I think vegetables are better for you.

1 _____

Yes, but I always thought I'd miss meat too much. The idea of being a vegetarian for 30 days was really good because I could give it a try and then see how I feel.

2 _____

No, I feel really good. Actually, I don't miss meat at all, so I think I'll easily manage the 30 days, and I might try to keep going longer.

**Challenge 2:
Carla decided to draw
something every day.**

Carla, why did you decide to draw something every day?

Well, I've never been very good at drawing, but I've always thought I'd like to start drawing things around me. It's one of those things that you think about doing, but you never actually do.

3 _____

All kinds of things. At the beginning, I drew objects around me at home. Then I went out on my lunch break and started drawing things outdoors, like yesterday I drew a duck in the park – that was really difficult!

So do you feel like it's been worthwhile?

Oh yes, definitely. I'm still not very good at drawing, but it's been a lot of fun and it's very relaxing.

c Complete the interviews with the missing questions.

a And who do you practice with? Or are you just working alone?

b Didn't you ever think of being a vegetarian before?

c And how do you feel? Are you finding it difficult?

d And do you think you'll keep going after the 30 days?

e What have you drawn pictures of so far?

d ▶ 01.11 Listen and check your answers.

**Challenge 3:
Steve decided to
learn Italian.**

Steve, what language did you decide to learn?

Well, I thought I'd choose a language that isn't too different from English, so I decided to try Italian.

Isn't it difficult to keep it up?

Yes, it is. I've had to be very strict with myself. I'm using a book with online support, so I usually try to cover one lesson a night.

4 _____

Well, there's an Italian restaurant nearby and I'm friends with the owner, so I go there and I talk to him. That's another reason I chose Italian.

5 _____

Maybe, or I might try a different language every month. I'm thinking of trying Japanese next.

4 GRAMMAR Questions

a Read the rules about questions. Find examples of each type of question in the interviews and 3c.

> 1 In questions, we usually put the auxiliary verb before the subject. If there is no auxiliary verb, we add *do* or *did*.
> **Are you** making dinner? **Have you** eaten?
> *What **did you** eat?*
>
> 2 If the question word (*who*, *what*, or *which*) is the subject, we keep normal word order.
> **Who spoke** to you? **What happened** next?
>
> 3 If a question has a preposition, it can come at the end:
> *You were talking to someone.* → *Who were you talking **to**?*
>
> 4 To ask an opinion, we often ask questions starting with a phrase like
> *Do you think … ?*
> *Is it a good idea?* → **Do you think** *it's a good idea?*

b Compare examples a and b.

a Did you see her at the party?   b Didn't you see her at the party?

Which example … ?

1 is a neutral question (= maybe she was there, maybe not)

2 expresses surprise (= I'm sure she was there)

c Compare examples c and d.

c Which color do you want?   d What color do you want?

Which example … ?

1 asks about an open choice (there may be a lot of colors to choose from)

2 asks about a limited range (e.g., black, red, or green)

d ≫ Now go to Grammar Focus 1B on p. 134.

e 💬 Work in pairs. You are going to role-play two of the interviews in 3b and continue with your own questions.

1 Choose one of the interviews.
   Student A: Interview Student B. Add your own questions.
   Student B: Answer Student A's questions using your own ideas.

2 Choose a second interview. This time Student B interviews Student A.

5 SPEAKING

a Work in pairs.

1 Write down three challenges you might do in the next three months.

   1 Write a short poem every day
   2 Get up at dawn
   3 Go running

2 Look at your partner's challenges. Write some questions to ask about each one. Ask about:
   • reasons for doing the challenge
   • details of what he/she plans to do
   • how he/she feels about it.

   Are you planning to … ?   Do you think it will be … ?

   How are you going to … ?

b 💬 Interview your partner about his/her three challenges. Do you think he/she will be successful?

1C EVERYDAY ENGLISH
Don't touch the food

1 LISTENING

a 💬🔊 Answer the questions.

1 In your country, how do students manage financially? Do they ... ?
- rely on their parents
- get a part-time job
- use student loans
2 What do you think is the best way? Why?
3 If you had to get a part-time job to earn some money as a student, what job would you choose and why?

b Look at the photo of Emma and Susana below. Who do you think they are?

1 tourists visiting a famous building
2 college students leaving a class
3 journalists who have just given an interview

c ▶ 01.14 Listen to Part 1 and check your ideas.

d ▶ 01.14 Listen again. Answer the questions.

1 Are Emma and Susana friends? How do you know?
2 Why does Susana have to go?

e ▶ 01.15 Listen to Part 2. Are these sentences true or false?

1 Susana and Tomás are roommates.
2 Susana is free this evening.
3 Susana is in a hurry.

2 CONVERSATION SKILLS
Cutting a conversation short

a Look at these ways to cut a conversation short and say goodbye.

1 I really have to go now.
2 I have to run.
3 I have no time to talk now.
4 I'll see you tomorrow.

▶ 01.16 Listen to the speaker. Which words does she not use in 1–4?

b Look at some more ways to cut a conversation short. Which words are not included?

1 Got to run now.
2 Talk to you later.
3 Can't talk now.
4 Nice talking to you.

Tomás

3 PRONUNCIATION Rapid speech

a ▶ 01.17 In rapid speech, we often leave out sounds. Listen to the phrases below. Which sound is left out? Is it a consonant sound or a vowel sound?

1 must go
2 got to run
3 got to go
4 can't talk

b Read the conversation. Put B's replies in order. Is more than one order possible?

A So how was your vacation?
B Got to go. / Sorry. / Can't talk now. / It was great.
A OK, well, have a nice evening.
B Bye. / See you tomorrow. / Yeah, thanks. / Must go now.

c 💬🔊 Work in pairs. Have short conversations.

Student A: Tell Student B about what you did last weekend. Continue until he/she stops you.
Student B: You're in a hurry. Use expressions in 2b and 3b to cut the conversation short.

Then switch roles.

Emma
Susana

Dave

4 LISTENING

a ▶ 01.18 Listen to Part 3. What happens to Susana? Choose the correct answer.

1 She does her homework in the café.
2 She learns how to do her job.

b ▶ 01.18 Listen again. Answer the questions.

1 Dave explains things to Susana. What are they?
2 What does Dave do in the café?

c 💬 Discuss the question with other students. Give reasons for your answers.

Do you think Susana will be good at her new job?

d ▶ 01.19 Listen to Part 4. Which of these topics do Susana and Tomás mention?

| coffee | food | Susana's new job | the reason Tomás is there |
| a test | a presentation | | |

e ▶ 01.19 Listen again. What do Tomás and Susana say about each topic?

5 USEFUL LANGUAGE
Explaining and checking understanding

a Look at the expressions Dave uses to explain what to do. Put the words in *italics* in the correct order.

1 *most / thing / is, / the / important* don't touch the food.
2 *to / always / remember* use these tongs.
3 *is, / remember / thing / to / another* the tables are all numbered.

b ▶ 01.20 Listen and check your answers.

c Why does Dave use these expressions?

1 because he needs time to think
2 because he's not sure
3 to emphasize important points

d Look at these ways to check that someone has understood an explanation. Complete the questions with the endings in the box.

| the idea? | get that? | clear? | I mean? |

1 Is that …   3 Did you …
2 Do you know what … 4 Do you get …

e ▶ 01.21 **Pronunciation** Listen to each question in 5d said two ways. Which way sounds … ?

• friendly and polite
• unfriendly and not so polite

To sound friendly, does the speaker's voice go up (↗) or down (↘) at the end?

f Practice asking the questions in 5d in a friendly and polite way.

g Here are some other things Dave could explain to Susana. Imagine what he could say using language in 5a and 5d. What could Susana say to show she has understood?

1 how to clear and arrange a table when a customer leaves
2 what to do with the coffee machine at closing time
3 what to do if customers leave something behind

h 💬 Practice the conversation in 5g. Switch roles.

6 SPEAKING

a Choose a process you are familiar with or something you know how to do. It could be:

• something connected with a sport or a hobby
• how to use a machine or an electronic device
• how to make or cook something.

b You are going to explain the process to your partner. Prepare what you will say. Think how to emphasize the important points and check that your partner understands. Use expressions from 5a and 5d.

c 💬 Work in pairs. Take turns explaining the process to your partner and ask each other questions to check understanding.

⟳ UNIT PROGRESS TEST

→ **CHECK YOUR PROGRESS**

You can now do the Unit Progress Test.

1 SPEAKING AND LISTENING

a 💬🔊 Discuss the questions.

1 In your daily life, how much do you depend on technology?
2 What aspects of technology make your daily life easier?

b 💬🔊 Look at the research results below and discuss the questions.

1 Do you think people you know would agree with these results?
2 Do you agree with the results? Is there anything you would add to the list?

IT Anxiety!

Recent research in the U.S. has revealed the things that make people the most anxious about information technology (IT). Here are the top five:

1 There is less face-to-face social contact.
2 IT companies know too much about us.
3 Artificial intelligence could mean job losses.
4 Too much time is wasted online.
5 Information online is often unreliable.

c ▶️ 01.22 Listen to Gina and Derek talking about technology. What aspect of technology do they talk about? Are they describing positive or negative experiences?

d ▶️ 01.22 Listen again. What's the speaker's relationship with the other person in the story? What made the experience positive or negative? Why?

e 💬🔊 Discuss the questions.

1 Do you agree with Gina's reaction to her boss? Why / Why not?
2 Do you know people like Derek? Do you think they should try to change? Why / Why not?

f Work on your own. Think about the questions below and take notes.

• When has technology created a problem for you?
• When has technology helped you solve a problem of some kind?

g 💬🔊 Discuss your experiences in 1f.

2 READING

a Read "Tech Free!" Did Sam have a really difficult day or some nice surprises?

b Read the text again. Are the sentences true or false?

1 Before the experiment, Sam was a little worried by the idea.
2 Sam was annoyed that he had to talk to someone in the bank.
3 The bank teller was surprised that Sam wanted to withdraw money.
4 Sam was able to work better when he wrote by hand.
5 As the day progressed, Sam thought less about using his phone.
6 The book he read made him fall asleep.
7 Sam learned something about the way we depend on technology.

c 💬🔊 How would you feel if you had to live without using technology for one day? Discuss what you would enjoy and not enjoy.

3 WRITING SKILLS
Organizing an article

a How does Sam organize his article? Choose the correct summary.

1 He explains his attitude toward technology, describes his day, requests readers to do the same thing.
2 He explains his level of dependency on technology, describes his day, finishes with an evaluation of the experience.
3 He explains his feelings about technology, describes his day, finishes by promising to repeat the experience.

b How does Sam get the reader's attention at the beginning of the article?

TECH FREE!

by Sam Winton

[1]Have you ever wondered what it would be like to give up technology? I'm a freelance marketing consultant, and I spend a lot of my working life in front of a computer. I've been working on a marketing campaign for this nature resort where any kind of digital device is banned. I wanted to know what it's like, so I decided to conduct my own private experiment: Spend a day without technological devices – scary!

[2]The first thing I usually do every day is reach for my cell phone to check the time and read any messages, but I'd locked it in a drawer the night before. Already I was feeling very cut off from the world, and it was only … actually, I had no idea what time it was!

[3]After breakfast, I needed to get some cash. Inevitably, this meant a trip to the bank teller because I couldn't use my card or an ATM. I had to stand in line at the bank, but I had a very nice conversation with a woman while I was waiting. She told me how they're going to upgrade the local park with a new playground and a running track. Not surprisingly, the bank teller thought I was a little strange to be making a cash withdrawal in person. Most people use machines.

[4]Afterward, I came home to try writing my marketing plan by hand. Interestingly, I found it easier to concentrate on my writing. But my hand got really sore from writing with a pen! And I have to confess – by this stage, I was having to make a real effort not to get my phone out and check my messages.

[5]Then, I wanted to relax and watch the next episode in a series that I'm streaming. Naturally, that was out – I had to read a book. It's a crime story a friend recommended to me, and it's great. I couldn't put it down and went to bed late.

[6]All in all, I wouldn't say I could live without technology. Predictably, I really missed my phone all day. However, I kept to my promise of a tech-free day and had more face-to-face interaction by avoiding machines. Undoubtedly, it made me realize just how addicted to technology we all are.

---

c Complete the tasks.

1 In paragraphs 2–5, underline the linking word or phrase that sequences the events in Sam's day. The first one has been done for you.

2 In paragraph 6, what linking phrase shows that Sam is going to summarize his experience?

d Look at the example sentence from the article.

Inevitably, this meant a trip to the bank teller because I couldn't use my card or an ATM.

The adverb *Inevitably* shows the writer's attitude. Find five other comment adverbs in the article.

e Add the adverbs in the box to the sentences. (There is more than one possible answer.)

amazingly   naturally   inevitably
(not) surprisingly

1 Why do some websites ask you to change passwords? _____, after changing the password for my bank, I was asked to change it again a week later.

2 I usually hate anything to do with technology. _____, I like using the self-service check-out at my local grocery store.

3 I always expect digital devices to be expensive. _____, the tablet I bought last week cost very little.

4 I find it very difficult to install new software. _____, I downloaded the new version of a program, and now my computer is frozen.

f Which piece of advice is not correct for writing an article? Why?

1 Begin the article with a question to get the reader's attention.
2 Use direct questions to connect with the reader of your article.
3 Think about how you can structure the main part of the article. You can use a sequence of events or you could compare and contrast ideas.
4 Use linking words to guide the reader.
5 Be as objective as possible.
6 Use comment adverbs to show your opinions.
7 Summarize your experience or ideas and evaluate them.

4 WRITING

a Imagine you had to live for a week without a technological device you use in your daily life. Choose a device from the article or use your own idea. Take notes about what the experience might be like.

b 💬 Discuss your notes.

c Write an article about your experience. Organize your article to follow the structure in 3a. Use the linking phrases and adverbs from 3c–e to help you.

d Switch articles with another student. Does the article follow the advice in 3f? Is the article interesting to read? Why? What could make it more interesting?

1 GRAMMAR

a Write verbs in the blanks in the correct tense.

My wife Anna and I first ¹_____ (meet) at a party while I ²_____ (live) in London in the 1970s. When I ³_____, (arrive) most people ⁴_____ (already/leave). I ⁵_____ (notice) Anna immediately. She ⁶_____ (wear) a blue dress, and she ⁷_____ (chat) with a group of people on the balcony. I ⁸_____ (go) up to her and we ⁹_____ (start) talking. We both ¹⁰_____ (feel) as if we ¹¹_____ (know) each other all our lives. Now we ¹²_____ (be) both in our 70s. We ¹³_____ (know) each other for 44 years.

b Read an interview with a famous actor about his life. Correct the mistakes in the questions.

1 *Where you grew up?*
   In San Diego, California. I left when I was 18.
2 *Did not you like living in San Diego?*
   Yes, but there were more opportunities in San Francisco.
3 *How long for did you stay there?*
   About eight years. Then I moved to New York.
4 *What did make you decide to move?*
   I got an offer to act at the Apollo Theater in New York.
5 *Do you think was it a good decision?*
   Oh, yes. It was a chance to work with some great people.
6 *Did you work with who?*
   Oh, a lot of good actors – Terence Newby, for example.

2 VOCABULARY

a Add an adjective to fill in the blanks.

1 The students are all eager to learn English. They're very m_____.
2 All Sophie's family and friends have warned her about marrying Fred, but she's going to anyway. She's so s_____.
3 Everyone agrees the new president is a good leader. She's highly r_____.
4 My brother used to be very shy, but he's become much more s_____ since he left home.
5 I've always loved acting more than anything else. I'm p_____ about it.
6 Five thousand people came to hear him talk. He's a very i_____ speaker.
7 Try not to criticize his work. He can be very s_____ about it.
8 Just because they're rich, they think they're better than everyone else. I hate a_____ people like that.

b Choose the correct answers.

1 I ¹*took / made* a chance at running a café, but it didn't work ²*up / out*. I didn't make enough money, so I had to ³*give / stop* up.
2 He's really ⁴*doing / making* an effort to lose weight. He's on a diet, and he's ⁵*kept / held* it up for six weeks now. But I don't know if he'll ⁶*make / stick* with it for much longer.
3 He saw a poster for a pottery class and decided to try it ⁷*out / on*. After two classes he managed ⁸*to / for* make a vase.

3 WORDPOWER *make*

a Match the statements with the pictures.

a "I can't make up my mind."
b "It really makes a difference to the room."
c "I can't make out what it is."
d "We'll have to make the best of it."
e "This is to make up for last night."
f "That doesn't make sense."
g "It wants to make friends with us."

b ▶ 01.23 Listen to the conversations and check your answers.

c Add a word or phrase from **a** after *make* in these sentences.

1 What was that? I can't make _____ what you're saying.
2 Why don't you drive faster? We need to make _____ lost time or we'll be late.
3 So do you want to come with us? You need to make _____.
4 When the sun shines, it makes _____ to the way I feel.
5 I didn't buy any more food. You'll just have to make _____ o
6 He gave a long explanation, but it didn't make _____ to me. I still don't understand.
7 Don't sit in front of the computer all day. You should go out and make _____ with people.

d 💬 What kind of person are you? Discuss these questions.

1 If you upset a friend, how would you make up for it? Would buy a present, buy flowers, apologize …?
2 When you buy clothes, do you make up your mind quickly or do you need a long time to decide?
3 You have to spend the night at an airport. Would you stay th and make the best of it or would you pay money for a hotel?
4 You see a dog in the street. Would you try to make friends w it or would you keep out of its way?

⟳ REVIEW YOUR PROGRESS

How well did you do in this unit? Write 3, 2, or 1 for each objective.
3 = very well   2 = well   1 = not so well

I CAN ...	
discuss people I admire	☐
discuss a challenge	☐
explain what to do and check understanding	☐
write an article.	☐

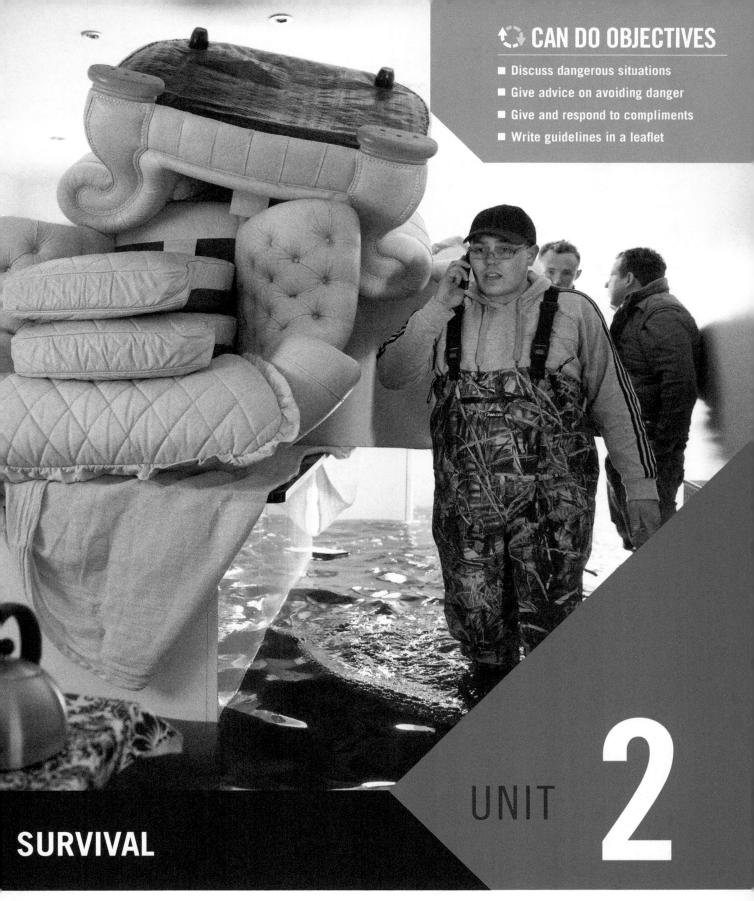

UNIT **2**

SURVIVAL

GETTING STARTED

a 💬🗨 Look at the picture and answer the questions.

1 What do you think has happened here?
2 Who are the people in the picture?
3 What's the man on the phone saying?

b 💬🗨 Discuss the questions.

1 What do you think are the worst kinds of natural disasters? Why?
2 Think of a natural disaster that has happened in your country. How effective was the response of the emergency services? How well did people cope?
3 Why do you think some people cope better with challenging situations than others?

2A | IT WAS GETTING LATE AND I WAS LOST

1 LISTENING

a Look at pictures a–d. What would you be most afraid of in each situation?

b ▶ 02.01 Listen to someone talking about their vacation. Which of the pictures is being described? Where was the vacation?

c ▶ 02.01 Listen again. Number events a–h in the order that they happened.

a ☐ bought a new surfboard
b ☐ lost the board
c ☐ waved to a lifeguard
d ☐ swam against the current
e ☐ fell off the surfboard
f ☐ learned to surf with instructors
g ☐ went surfing alone
h ☐ was rescued

2 VOCABULARY Expressions with *get*

a Match expressions 1–10 in **bold** with meanings a–j.

1 ☐ I can't wait to **get away**.
2 ☐ I've always wanted to learn how to surf, and I'll finally **get to** do it.
3 ☐ I **couldn't get over** just how strong they are.
4 ☐ Actually, I **got into** a little **trouble** once.
5 ☐ I tried to **get hold of** it.
6 ☐ It **got swept away** by the wave.
7 ☐ I soon realized that I **wasn't getting anywhere**.
8 ☐ I **got the feeling** I was being pulled out to sea.
9 ☐ So I waved to **get someone's attention**.
10 ☐ I had a bad experience, but I soon **got over** it.

a make no progress
b move in a different direction in a powerful way
c have the chance to do something
d go somewhere else
e be very surprised by something
f find myself in difficulty
g take it in my hand
h recover from something negative that happened
i make someone notice
j have the sensation that

b Complete the sentences with the correct form of the phrases in 2a. Write one word in each blank.

1 She ran out on the road to _____ the police officer's _____.
2 They were exhausted and hungry, but after some food and sleep they soon _____ _____ the experience.
3 When he saw the same tree for the third time, he began to _____ _____ _____ that he was lost.
4 He took a class about surviving in the woods and _____ _____ put into practice his fire-making skills.
5 They decided to ski off the main trail where the snow was fresh, but it was also very dangerous and they soon _____ _____ _____.
6 The boat was sinking, but we all managed to _____ _____ _____ a life jacket.
7 She was crossing the river, but the current was strong and she _____ _____ _____ by the water.
8 They had been walking for hours, but they'd only walked about two kilometers. They felt like they weren't _____ _____.
9 They were in such a rush to _____ _____ to the mountains, they left without taking hiking boots.
10 When they were in the water, they _____ _____ _____ how high the waves were.

c ≫ Now go to Vocabulary Focus on p. 155.

3 READING

a Read the article "Lost at Sea" and answer the questions.

1 How long was Robert Hewitt in the water?
2 What problems did he have to overcome?

b Can you remember what these numbers refer to? Write sentences about each number. Then read the text again and check your answers.

1 200-meter
2 seven kilometers
3 fourth day
4 three hours
5 half a kilometer
6 third day

c 💬 Answer the questions.

1 What do you think most helped Robert to survive?
2 Do you think that Robert made the right decision on day one not to try to swim for shore? Give reasons.
3 What was the biggest challenge Robert had to overcome?
4 What would you have done in Robert's situation?

REAL DIVING

Stories   Locations   Learn to Dive   Shop

LOST AT SEA

How long could you survive at sea? One day? Two? And when would you start to lose hope?

When Robert Hewitt came to the surface, he [1]**realized** right away that something was wrong. He [2]**'d been diving** for sea urchins and crayfish off the coast of New Zealand with a friend, and [3]**had decided** to make the 200-meter swim back to shore alone. But instead, strong underwater currents had taken him more than half a kilometer out to sea.

Lying on his back in the middle of the ocean, Robert told himself not to panic. He was a strong swimmer and he [4]**was wearing** his thick wetsuit. "I'm not going to die. Someone will come," he told himself. But three hours passed and still no one had come for him. Robert would soon have to make a tough decision.

He was now a long way from the coast, and the tide was taking him further out, but he decided not to try to swim for shore. He felt it was better to save his energy and hold on to his brightly colored equipment. But the decision was not an easy one. "I just closed my eyes and said, 'You've made the right decision. You've made the right decision' until that's all I heard," he remembers.

As night approached, Robert established a pattern to help him survive in the water. To stay warm, he kept himself moving and took short naps of less than a minute at a time. Every few hours, he called out to his loved ones, "Just yelling out their names would pick me up, and then I would keep going for the next hour and the next hour and the next."

When he woke up the next morning, he couldn't believe he was still alive. Using his bright equipment, he tried to signal to planes that flew overhead. But as each plane turned away, his spirits dropped. He managed to drink rainwater that he collected in his mask to keep himself alive, but as day turned to night again, he started to imagine things.

Robert woke up on the third day to a beautiful blue sky. Now seven kilometers off the coast, Robert decided he had to swim for it. But the sun was so strong and Robert quickly ran out of strength. Hope turned to disappointment yet again. "I felt disappointed in myself. I thought I was a lot fitter. I thought I would be able to do it." Robert then started to think he might not survive.

On the fourth day, the lack of food and water was really starting to affect him. Half unconscious, and with strange visions going through his head, he thought he saw a boat coming toward him with two of his friends on board. Another vision, surely.

But no: "They put me in the boat and I said something like, 'Oh, how's it going, what are you guys doing here?'" Then he asked them the question that he'd asked in all his visions, "Can I have some water?" As they handed him the water and he felt it touch his lips, he knew. This was not a vision. He'd been found! After four days and three nights alone at sea, Robert had been found! Sunburned, hungry, and exhausted, but alive …

GLOSSARY

sea urchin

crayfish

4 GRAMMAR Narrative tenses

a Look at the verbs in **bold** in "Lost at Sea" and match them with the uses a–d.

  a a completed action that takes place before the main events in the story

  b a background action in progress at the same time as the main events in the story happened

  c a continuous activity that happens before the main events in the story and explains why the main events happen

  d a completed action that tells you what happens at a specific time in the story

b ▶02.05 **Pronunciation** Listen to the three sentences. Underline the stressed verb in each sentence. How do we pronounce the words *had been*? Listen again and repeat.

He *had been* diving for seafood.
He *had been* swimming in the sea.
He *had been* wearing a wetsuit.

c ≫ Now go to Grammar Focus 2A on p. 136.

d Work in pairs. Student A: Read about Eric LeMarque. Student B: Read about Ricky Megee. Answer the questions about your text.

  1 Where does the event take place?
  2 Does the person survive?

e Underline the correct verbs in your text.

f You are going to tell your partner about your story. Take notes.

g 💬 Tell your partner your survival story. Use correct verb forms.

5 SPEAKING

a Think of a dangerous situation that you or someone you know was in, or it could be something you know about from a book or movie. Take notes about the questions.

- Where and when did it take place?
- Who was involved?
- What was the scene or background to the story?
- What were the main events?
- How did you / the person feel?
- What was the outcome?

b 💬 Tell each other your story. Use different narrative tenses and expressions with *get*. Ask questions.

Student A: ERIC LEMARQUE

It was getting late, and Eric LeMarque decided to have one final run on his snowboard. As he [1]*'d gone / was going* down the mountain, he [2]*came / was coming* across some thick fog and headed in the wrong direction. All of a sudden, he was completely lost. All he had with him was his snowboard, some bubble gum, and an MP3 player. Eventually, he [3]*remembered / 'd remembered* something he [4]*was seeing / 'd seen* in a movie about using an MP3 player as a compass. This meant he was able to get an idea of where he was and head in the right direction, up the mountain. Eric was missing for a week. During that time, he fell in a river, almost went down a waterfall, and had to walk through snow that was four and a half meters deep! On the eighth day, he was seen by a helicopter that [5]*had searched / had been searching* for him. He was completely exhausted but alive.

Student B: RICKY MEGEE

A farmer couldn't believe it when he found a strange man living in the Australian bush. Ricky Megee [1]*lived / had been living* off the land for over two months. It's unclear how Ricky ended up in the bush, but he claimed he [2]*had been driving / had driven* when he [3]*stopped / had stopped* to help some people whose car had broken down. He said the people stole his car and he was left alone and lost in the bush. According to his story, he [4]*ate / had eaten* insects, snakes, and frogs before he eventually found a pond with water. He built a small shelter and waited until he was rescued. The mystery of the stolen car and robbers was never solved, and some people didn't believe the story of how Ricky got there, but one thing seemed to be true. He survived for 71 days in the bush, and by the time he was discovered, he [5]*'d lost / was losing* more than 50 kg.

1 READING

a 💬 Think of three wild places.

- Would you be scared to go for a walk there?
- What dangers could you face?
- What would you do to get out of danger?

b 💬 Look at pictures a–e and answer the questions.

1 Which of the animals do you think are the most and least dangerous?
2 How good do you think your chances are of surviving an attack by these animals?

c Read the text and check your answers.

d Read the text again. Check (✓) the correct sentences.

1 ☐ Some animals are less dangerous than people think.
2 ☐ If you go walking, you can't avoid meeting dangerous animals.
3 ☐ Not many animals attack without reason.
4 ☐ Having a weapon may help you survive an attack.
5 ☐ Most animals have a part of their body that is vulnerable.
6 ☐ It's better to run away than to try to fight.

e Do you think the text is … ?

a a serious survival guide for travelers
b part of a scientific book about animals
c an article written mainly for interest and amusement

How to Survive...
an Animal Attack

YOU'RE WALKING IN A FOREST WHEN SUDDENLY A WILD ANIMAL APPEARS FROM NOWHERE AND IT DOESN'T LOOK FRIENDLY. WHAT DO YOU DO?

The first important point is that there's not usually much you can do, except hope it goes away again. With luck, you may never have to defend yourself against a wild animal, but it doesn't hurt to know what to do if an escaped leopard attacks you in your backyard, or if you're going for a country walk and you suddenly meet a pack of wolves.

BE AWARE
The first thing is to know which animals are really dangerous. Many people are scared of animals that are in fact harmless, and not scared enough of animals that could kill you. Most animals won't attack people unless you do something to make them angry. Bears, for example, will usually move away as soon as they hear you, and they'll only fight if they think you're attacking them or their young. Wolves won't normally attack unless they are very hungry, and then only if they're in a group. Tarantulas are big, hairy spiders, but they aren't actually dangerous at all – you can keep them as pets. On the other hand, tigers and crocodiles are serious killers who will be happy to eat you for breakfast.

BE PREPARED
It's a good idea to take a stick, knife, or pepper spray when you go for a walk in the wild in case you meet a dangerous animal. Have it in a place where you can easily find it. It may mean the difference between life and death.

KNOW YOUR ENEMY
If you ever find yourself face-to-face with a large and dangerous animal, you'll want to know their strong and weak points. Common weak points are:

- the nose
- the eyes
- the neck.

People have sometimes survived by punching sharks, large cats, and crocodiles on the nose, and pushing your thumbs into their eyes will also work well, as long as you press hard enough. Otherwise, you might just make them angry!

You can also try to get a psychological advantage. Provided you seem bigger and more dangerous than the animal, it will probably leave you alone, so make a lot of noise and try to make yourself look bigger.

WHAT NEXT?
If scaring them doesn't work, then you have two options: running or fighting. Remember that most animals are better at running and fighting than humans, so don't expect things to end well. But if you decide to fight, fight back with everything you have. Often during animal attacks, people give up before the fight has even started. If you have any sharp objects or weapons, then use them. Hit the animal's weak points, keep shouting, and make sudden movements. Good luck out there!

f Look at the ideas below for surviving attacks by three different animals. For each animal, decide which ideas are the best. More than one answer is possible.

g ⟫ **Communication 2B** Now go to p. 127 to check your answers.

1 A wolf
a hit it on the nose with a stick
b look it straight in the eyes
c run away immediately

2 A shark
a swim away quickly
b swim toward it
c hit it in the eye if it bites you

3 A bear
a run straight uphill as fast as you can
b lie down and "play dead"
c hit the trees with sticks if you think bears are nearby

2 GRAMMAR Future time clauses and conditionals

a Look at the words and phrases in **bold** in sentences 1–5 and answer questions a–e.

1 They'll only fight **if** they think you're attacking them.
2 They won't attack people **unless** they're trapped or provoked.
3 Bears, for example, will usually move away **as soon as** they hear you.
4 **Provided** you stay absolutely still, the bear will lose interest and go away.
5 **As long as** you don't panic, it will probably swim away.

a Which two words or phrases have a similar meaning to *if*?
b What does sentence 2 mean?
   1 A bear will only attack you if it's trapped or provoked.
   2 A bear will attack you anyway, even if it isn't trapped.
c What does sentence 3 mean?
   1 When bears hear you they will wait, then move away slowly.
   2 When bears hear you they will move away immediately.
d Look at these examples:
   If you stay still, the bear will go away
   (= something good will happen).
   If you move, the bear will attack you
   (= something bad will happen).
   In which example could we use *as long as* or *provided* instead of *if*?
e What tense is used after the words and phrases in **bold**? What tense is used in the other part of the sentence?

b Find one more example in "How to Survive ... an Animal Attack" of each of these words and phrases:

1 as long as
2 unless
3 provided.

c ⟫ Now go to Grammar Focus 2B on p. 136.

d Complete the sentences. There is more than one possible answer. Compare with other students.

1 Sharks won't attack you unless …
2 Wolves will only attack if …
3 A stick may help you provided …
4 If you hit a crocodile on the nose, …

3 LISTENING AND VOCABULARY
Animals and the environment

a 💬🔊 *The Tiger* by John Vaillant tells the true story of a hunter and a Siberian tiger. Use the words in the box to guess what the story is about.

tiger	mattress	attacked
hut	forest	wounded	shot
killed	boots	

b ▶️02.10 Listen to an interview about the book. Was the story similar to yours?

c ▶️02.10 Which of these questions *doesn't* Miles answer? Listen again and check.

1 Is a Siberian tiger bigger than other tigers?
2 How far can it jump?
3 Have many people been killed by Siberian tigers?
4 Can tigers plan ahead?

d ▶️02.11 Listen to the second part of the interview. Check (✓) the things Miles talks about.

1 ☐ his own feelings about the tiger
2 ☐ life in Siberia
3 ☐ the relationship between humans and tigers
4 ☐ tigers as an endangered species
5 ☐ how to survive a tiger attack

e 💬🔊 Do you think Miles would agree with statements 1–5? Write *Yes* or *No*. Then explain why.

1 It's a good thing they killed the tiger. _____
2 The tiger was just behaving naturally. _____
3 Tigers have always caused problems for people in Siberia. _____
4 In some ways, humans are more dangerous than tigers. _____
5 We should hunt more tigers to keep them under control. _____

f Which of the words in the box can we use to describe … ?

1 animals   2 places

at risk	creature	endangered	environment	extinct
habitats	hunt	natural	protected	rare	species

g ▶️02.12 Complete the sentences with the words in 3f. Then listen and check your answers.

1 Eastern Siberia is one of the wildest and most _____ _____ for tigers on Earth.
2 Imagine a/an _____ that is as active as a cat and has the weight of an industrial refrigerator.
3 Humans and tigers _____ the same animals and share the same _____.
4 Tigers are _____ because of humans.
5 Tigers have become extremely _____.
6 There are many more humans than tigers, so they really are an _____ _____, and although they're _____, they could easily become _____ in a few decades.

4 SPEAKING

a A visitor is coming to stay in your country. Take notes about:

• endangered species and where you can see them
• dangerous animals or other creatures (e.g., birds, fish, insects)
• other possible risks or dangers (e.g., diseases, dangerous places, travel, weather).

b Imagine what you could tell the visitor and what advice you could give. How could you use the words in the box?

if	as soon as	in case	unless	as long as	provided

c 💬🔊 Work in pairs. Student A, talk about your country. Student B, you are the visitor. Ask Student A questions. Then change roles.

> Take malaria pills in case you get bitten by a mosquito.

> Be careful of dogs if you go jogging.

2C EVERYDAY ENGLISH
What an amazing apartment!

Learn to give and respond to compliments
- S Giving compliments and responding
- P Agreeing using question tags

1 LISTENING

a 💬📱 Discuss the questions.

1 Do you like trying new kinds of food? Why / Why not?
2 In your opinion, what makes a good meal?
3 Do you know how to cook? Have you ever cooked a meal for your family or friends?

b Look at the photo and answer the questions.

1 What kind of food is shown?
2 How do you think it is prepared?

c ▶02.13 Listen to Part 1. Check your answers.

d ▶02.13 Are the sentences true or false? Listen again to check.

1 Esther tells Maya how to prepare the food.
2 Esther says that the meat is usually eaten raw.
3 Maya likes the food.
4 Esther says the food needs less sauce.

2 CONVERSATION SKILLS Agreeing using question tags

a ▶02.13 Listen again. How does Esther respond to Maya's comment, "It cooks quickly, doesn't it?"

b Choose the correct word.

1 We can use statements with question tags to *agree / disagree* with someone.
2 Using a different adjective in the answer is more *interesting / friendly*.

c Complete B's answers with the correct verb forms.

1 **A** I think she's a delightful person.
  B Yes, she's very charming, _____ she?
2 **A** Their instructions weren't very clear.
  B No, they weren't helpful, _____ they?

d Complete the rule with *affirmative* or *negative*.

If the sentence is affirmative, we use a/an _____ tag.
If the sentence is negative, we use a/an _____ tag.

e Complete B's replies. Use the adjectives in the box in the first blank and the correct verb form in the second blank.

welcoming ˙ soaking   breathtaking   worried

1 **A** Your clothes are all wet.
  B Yes, they're _____, _____ they?
2 **A** The scenery there is exceptional.
  B Yes, it's _____, _____ it?
3 **A** They weren't a very friendly group of people.
  B No, they weren't _____ at all, _____ they?
4 **A** He looks a little anxious.
  B Yes, he looks _____, _____ he?

3 PRONUNCIATION Intonation in question tags

a ▶02.14 Listen to the examples. Does the intonation go up (↗) or down (↘) on the question tag? What's the difference in meaning?

1 No, it isn't very fast, is it?
2 No, they weren't helpful, were they?
3 Yes, you need to make things easy, don't you?

b 💬📱 Practice the conversations in 2e.
Try to use the correct intonation in the reply.

c 💬📱 Discuss people and things you and other students know – for example, a person, a café, a movie, or a car. Use the adjectives below and question tags to agree.

- amusing – funny
- cheerful – happy
- interesting – fascinating
- frightening – terrifying
- exhausting – tiring

> That photo is really amazing.

> Yes, it's impressive, isn't it?

4 LISTENING

a Look at the photo of the apartment buildings. Which floor do you think the photo is taken from? How can you tell?

b Look at the two photos below. What are Maya and Esther eating this time?

c ▶ 02.15 Listen to Part 2. Where are Maya and Esther?

d ▶ 02.15 Listen to Part 2 again. Answer the questions.
1 What did Maya just finish doing?
2 How does Maya describe the food?
3 How does Esther feel about cooking?
4 Where do they go for dessert?

5 USEFUL LANGUAGE
Giving compliments and responding

a ▶ 02.16 Listen and complete the conversation.

MAYA Wow! What an _____ apartment, Esther!
ESTHER _____. It's all _____, I guess.
MAYA Oh, you have a _____ view.
ESTHER _____, after you walk _____ _____ floors.

b Answer the questions about the conversation.
1 Do Maya's compliments sound excited?
2 Are Esther's responses grateful or neutral?

c Look at the **bold** words in compliments 1–4. Match them to the words and phrases in a–d.

1 That was **excellent**!
2 You're so **good** about working out.
3 I **love** that you know where the best places are.
4 You really **managed to** get it just right.

a motivated / dedicated
b incredible / amazing / delicious
c were able to / succeeded in
d really like / am impressed

d Which of these responses are grateful and which are neutral?

Do you think so?

It's OK, I guess.

Thanks, I'm glad you like it.

I'm really pleased you like it.

e 💬 Work in pairs. Imagine you have both finished writing an essay and have read each other's essays. Use the ideas below to have a short conversation. Take turns being A and B.

A

Tell your partner how easy/difficult it was to write the essay.

Say you've read your partner's essay and compliment him/her.

B

Agree with A using a question tag.

Respond gratefully.

6 SPEAKING

a Work alone. What compliments can you give to your classmates? Think about:
- things they do or make as hobbies
- their jobs
- things they have done in your English classes
- the clothes they are wearing.

b 💬 Talk to different students in your class. Give compliments and respond.

That's a really nice sweater you're wearing.

Thanks. It's not bad, is it?

✓ UNIT PROGRESS TEST
→ CHECK YOUR PROGRESS

You can now do the Unit Progress Test.

2D SKILLS FOR WRITING
Make sure you know where you're going

Learn to write guidelines in a leaflet

G Organizing guidelines in a leaflet

1 SPEAKING AND LISTENING

a 💬🗨 Discuss the questions.

1 When was the last time you went to some kind of natural environment?
2 What did you do there?
3 How did you prepare for your trip?

b ▶ 02.17 Listen to Luiza talk about an experience she had in Canada. Answer the questions.

1 Which natural environment does she talk about?
2 Near the beginning, she says, "I got in trouble." What was the trouble?

c ▶ 02.17 Listen again and answer the questions.

1 Why did Luiza get lost?
2 How did she decide which way to go?
3 What helped her find the clearing?

d 💬🗨 At the end, Luiza says, "I suddenly had the strange feeling I was not alone." What do you think happened next? Discuss your ideas.

e ▶ 02.18 Listen to the rest of Luiza's story. Were your ideas correct?

f ▶ 02.18 Listen again. Are the sentences true or false?

1 Luiza knew what to do.
2 She felt calm and wasn't afraid.
3 The helicopter saw Luiza the first time it flew over.
4 Luiza was surprised to find out she was close to the main trail.

g 💬🗨 What would you have done in Luiza's situation?

2 READING

a 💬🗨 Think about Luiza's experience. Imagine you are going hiking in a forest. What do you need to remember in order to be safe?

b Read the leaflet "Be Wise and Survive!" Were your ideas similar? Put headings in spaces A–C in the leaflet. There is one extra heading.

1 In the forest
2 If you get lost
3 Identifying useful plants
4 Preparation

c Read the leaflet again. What should you … ?

1 take with you when you go hiking
2 not do when you are hiking
3 do about food and drink if you are lost
4 do if you are lost: move around or stay in one place

desert

beach

forest

mountains

BE WISE AND SURVIVE!

We all enjoy being in the great outdoors. There are lots of amazing environments, but some of them can be quite challenging, even dangerous, and it's important that you think about safety. Here are some simple guidelines to help you stay safe.

A _____

1 Get a map of the area and make sure you know where you are going.
2 Check the weather forecast.
3 Wear clothes and shoes that are suitable for the conditions. If you think the weather may change suddenly, take extra clothing.
4 If you are going on a longer walk, take some emergency food with you.

B _____

5 Provided you follow the signs, you shouldn't get into trouble.
6 Never take shortcuts unless you're absolutely sure where they go.
7 Allow plenty of time to get to your destination or get back before it gets dark.

C _____

8 As soon as you realize you're lost, stop, keep calm, and plan what you will do next.
9 Don't eat all your food at once. Have a little at a time.
10 Try to find a source of water you can drink from, like a river or a stream. Being able to drink is more important than being able to eat.
11 Don't keep moving around. Find somewhere that is dry and get plenty of rest. It's easier for rescuers to find you if you stay in one place.
12 Always try to stay warm. You can cover yourself with dry plants.
13 If you need to keep moving, make sure you use rocks or pieces of wood as signs that show rescuers where you are going.
14 As long as you tell yourself you'll survive, you probably will!

3 WRITING SKILLS
Organizing guidelines in a leaflet

a Notice these verb forms used in the leaflet.
  1 **Check** the weather forecast. – affirmative imperative
  2 **Don't eat** all your food at once. – negative imperative
  3 **Never take** shortcuts … – frequency adverb + imperative
  4 **If** you **think** the weather may change suddenly, **take** extra clothing. – if + present tense + imperative

Find one more example of each verb form in the leaflet.

b Choose the correct answers.
  1 What's the function of the verb forms in 3a?
    a to give advice
    b to make indirect suggestions
  2 Why are those forms used?
    a to make the information clear and direct
    b to show hikers they have a strong obligation

c Correct the incorrect sentences.
  1 Not eat any plants you don't recognize.
  2 Never leave the group of people you are hiking with.
  3 If you will hear a rescue team, make a lot of noise.
  4 Always carries a pocket knife.
  5 As soon as it starts getting dark, stop and think about what to do next.
  6 If you have a map, take it with you.

4 WRITING

a Choose one of the situations in the box and take notes on advice you could include in a leaflet.

> camping in a forest   backpacking in a foreign country
> swimming in the ocean   hiking in the mountains

b Write a leaflet for the situation you chose above. Remember to:
  • use headings
  • include the different imperative forms in 3a
  • make the information clear and direct.

c Switch leaflets with another student. Does the leaflet include headings and different imperative forms? Is the information clear and direct? What improvements could be made?

d 💬 Give your leaflet to other students. Read other leaflets and decide which leaflet you think is the clearest and the most useful.

UNIT 2
Review and extension

1 GRAMMAR

a Complete the text with the verbs in parentheses. Use the simple past, past continuous, past perfect, or past perfect continuous forms.

The first time I ^{1}_____ (try) scuba diving ^{2}_____ (be) when I ^{3}_____ (live) in Costa Rica. I ^{4}_____ (travel) around Central America and I ^{5}_____ (decide) to stop and work for a few months. I ^{6}_____ (be) on a break between finishing college and beginning my career. Years before, someone ^{7}_____ (tell) me the best way to see the ocean ^{8}_____ (be) by scuba diving. The diving I ^{9}_____ (do) in Costa Rica ^{10}_____ (be) amazing. As I ^{11}_____ (dive), I ^{12}_____ (see) spectacular marine life.

b Make sentences by matching the halves. Put the connecting expression in parentheses in the correct place.

1 ☐ you won't find it difficult to learn to ski
2 ☐ you won't make much progress
3 ☐ you'll make steady progress
4 ☐ you won't be able to control your skis
5 ☐ you'll stay warm
6 ☐ you'll start making progress after a week

a   you can move your toes in your boots   (unless)
b   you're generally fit and healthy   (if)
c   you keep moving   (provided)
d   you choose an easy ski slope   (as long as)
e   you're patient with yourself   (provided)
f   you're prepared to fall down a lot at first (unless)

2 VOCABULARY

a Correct the errors in the sentences.

1   I dropped my hat in the ocean and it got swept by a wave away.
2   She couldn't get it over how hot it was.
3   He got trouble for being late.
4   I got feeling they didn't like guests.
5   She's now getting over it the shock of losing her job last week.
6   They're planning to get to the countryside this weekend.

b Complete the words.

1   In North America, red wolves are considered an
    e _ _ _ _ _ _ _ _ _ s _ _ _ _ _ _.
2   In the UK, large blue butterflies are a _ r _ _ _ and are p _ _ _ _ _ _ _ _.
3   The South American Spix's Macaw, featured in the movie *Rio*, is now e _ _ _ _ _ _ in the wild.
4   It's possible to find many Chinese alligators in zoos and research centers, but there are fewer living in their n _ _ _ _ _ h _ _ _ _ _ _ _.
5   In Australia, just over 20 percent of the native plants are considered r _ _ _ and need to be conserved.

3 WORDPOWER *face*

a Match examples 1–8 with definitions a–h.

1 ☐ Although he said he enjoys the taste of raw fish, he still **made a face**.
2 ☐ She **faced a difficult choice** between the two jobs she was offered.
3 ☐ Her **face fell** when I told her the painting was worthless.
4 ☐ I've been studying all day, and I **can't face** doing my homework now.
5 ☐ It's not good news, but I feel I need to **say it to his face**.
6 ☐ We just have to **face the fact** that we don't have enough money to buy a house.
7 ☐ I tripped on a loose brick and **fell flat on my face**.
8 ☐ I could tell my boss wasn't happy about the outcome. Now I have to talk to her and **face the music**.

a   to be disappointed
b   to accept another person's criticism or displeasure
c   to accept an unpleasant situation
d   to show from your expression that you don't like something
e   to fall down badly and feel embarrassed
f   to make a tough decision
g   to say something directly to someone
h   to not want to do something unpleasant

b In which of the expressions in 1–8 is *face* used as a noun and in which as a verb?

c Which one of the following nouns doesn't collocate with *face*?

1 a problem   2 the truth   3 a difficult decision
4 the facts   5 a success   6 reality

d Add words to the blanks.

1   When did you last fall _____ on your face?
2   What was the last _____ choice you had to face?
3   What happened the last time you saw someone's face _____?
4   What's something difficult you've had to say _____ someone's face?
5   What food causes you to _____ a face when you eat it?
6   When was the last time you had to face _____ music?

e 💬 Ask and answer the questions in 3d.

🔄 REVIEW YOUR PROGRESS

How well did you do in this unit? Write 3, 2, or 1 for each objective.
3 = very well   2 = well   1 = not so well

I CAN . . .	
discuss dangerous situations	☐
give advice on avoiding danger	☐
give and respond to compliments	☐
write guidelines in a leaflet.	☐

↻ **CAN DO OBJECTIVES**

■ Discuss ability and achievement
■ Discuss sports activities and issues
■ Make careful suggestions
■ Write a description of data

UNIT 3

TALENT

GETTING STARTED

a 💬🗪 Look at the picture and answer the questions.
1 What are the people doing?
2 Why do you think three people are needed for the job?
3 What could the woman be thinking?

b 💬🗪 Discuss the questions.
1 What makes something a work of art?
2 Do famous artists have natural talent? Or is their success due to luck, hard work, or something else? Why do you think so?

3A | I'M NOT VERY GOOD IN THE MORNING

Learn to discuss ability and achievement
- **G** Multi-word verbs
- **V** Ability and achievement

1 LISTENING

a 💬 Think about how to learn something new. Do you agree or disagree with sentences 1–5? Why?

1 Don't make mistakes in front of your teacher.
2 Children learn faster than adults.
3 Practice every day in order to make progress.
4 If something seems too easy, you must be doing it wrong.
5 Long practice sessions are best.

b ▶ 03.01 Listen to an experienced teacher talk about the same sentences. Are his ideas similar to yours? Do you agree with his ideas?

2 READING

a 💬 Discuss the questions.

1 How long does it take to learn something well?
2 What's the best time of day to learn something new?
3 What techniques do people use to help remember things?

b Read "Learning to Learn." Match texts a–c with the questions in 2a.

c Read questions 1–6 from people who have to learn something. Use information in the texts to answer the questions.

1 I have to learn a lot of historical dates for an exam. What's a good way to do this?
2 I want to join a beginners' kickboxing class. Is it better to join the morning or afternoon class?
3 I know I have a natural talent for tennis. Do I need to practice hard to do well?
4 If I study first thing in the morning after my brain has rested, I'm sure I'll learn more. Do you agree?
5 I have to find out about the way car engines work, but the book I'm reading is really boring. Should I just stick with it?
6 I don't just want to be a good computer programmer – I want to be an extraordinary one. What can I do to achieve that?

d 💬 Discuss the questions.

1 What information in the texts surprised you?
2 What information made sense to you?
3 Have you had any experience of the ideas discussed in the text?
4 Do you think you'll change your learning practice as a result of the information?

LEARNING TO LEARN

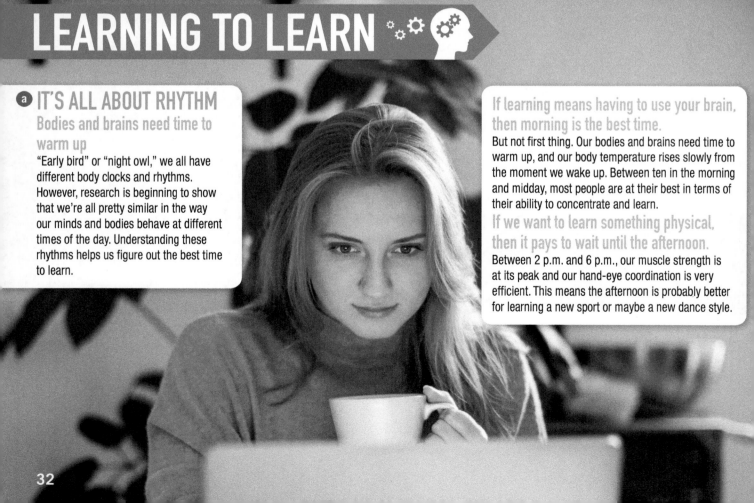

a IT'S ALL ABOUT RHYTHM
Bodies and brains need time to warm up

"Early bird" or "night owl," we all have different body clocks and rhythms. However, research is beginning to show that we're all pretty similar in the way our minds and bodies behave at different times of the day. Understanding these rhythms helps us figure out the best time to learn.

If learning means having to use your brain, then morning is the best time.
But not first thing. Our bodies and brains need time to warm up, and our body temperature rises slowly from the moment we wake up. Between ten in the morning and midday, most people are at their best in terms of their ability to concentrate and learn.

If we want to learn something physical, then it pays to wait until the afternoon.
Between 2 p.m. and 6 p.m., our muscle strength is at its peak and our hand-eye coordination is very efficient. This means the afternoon is probably better for learning a new sport or maybe a new dance style.

3 VOCABULARY
Ability and achievement

a Look at the adjectives in **bold** and answer questions 1–4.

And when you look at all the people who are **outstanding** at what they do …

… they seem so much more **talented** …

… that's what it takes to become really **skilled**.

Those who became **exceptional** practiced about 2,000 hours more …

… in order to learn something and become very **successful** at doing it, all you'll need is about 10,000 hours!

Without a doubt, there are people who are **extraordinary** at certain things …

All the musicians in the study had the **potential** to become world famous …

1 Which two adjectives describe a good level of ability?
2 Which adjective describes a good level of achievement?
3 Which three adjectives describe a very high level of ability or achievement?
4 Look at the noun in **bold** in the last sentence. Are the musicians world famous now or are they likely to be in the future?

b Write the noun forms of the adjectives.

1 skilled _____
2 talented _____
3 successful _____
4 able _____

c Complete the sentences with the words in the box.

| at   for   to (x2) |

1 He's very talented _____ playing the guitar.
2 He has a lot of potential _____ succeed in his career.
3 She's got a real talent _____ drawing.
4 She has the ability _____ become an exceptional actor.

d Think of an example of someone who:

1 is skilled at some kind of sport or art
2 has a talent for some kind of musical instrument
3 is famous and you think is extraordinary
4 is exceptional in their field
5 is the most successful person you know.

e 💬 Tell each other about your answers in 3d. Give reasons for your opinions.

b GIVE ME STRENGTH
A new word suggests a picture

Isn't it strange how we can remember the words of a much-loved poem that we learned in elementary school more than twenty years ago, but we can't remember where we left our keys about ten minutes ago? More than 130 years ago, this problem caught the attention of the German psychologist Hermann Ebbinghaus, and he came up with a theory: the strength of memory.

Ebbinghaus believed that if we find new information interesting, then it'll probably be more meaningful to us. This makes the information easier to learn and also helps the strength of memory. It also helps if we associate the new information with something else. For example, a new word we learn might make us think of a picture. This association can also build memory strength.

Using associations to help us remember what we learn is known as "mnemonics." For example, some people are able to remember a long sequence of numbers because the shape of all those numbers reminds them of a specific physical shape, such as a guitar. Mnemonic techniques are often used by competitors in the World Memory Championships held every year.

Popular spelling mnemonics:
BECAUSE
　Big Elephants Can't Always
　Use Small Exits
HERE or HEAR?
　We hear with our ear

c A QUESTION OF TALENT?
"All you'll need is about 10,000 hours!"

We've all had the experience of trying to learn something new only to find out that we're not very good at it. We look around at other people we're learning with who seem more talented and are doing so much better. It seems to come naturally to them. And when you look at all the people who are outstanding at what they do – the really famous people who are superstars – all you see is natural ability. The conclusion seems obvious: talented people must be born that way.

Without a doubt, there are people who are extraordinary at certain things – they have a talent for kicking a ball around a field, or they pick up a violin and immediately make music. However, there's also a lot to be said for practice. Psychologist K. Anders Ericsson studied students at Berlin's Academy of Music. He found that even though all the musicians in the study had the potential to become world famous, only some of them actually did. What made the difference? The answer is simple: time. Those who became exceptional were more competitive and practiced about 2,000 hours more than those who only did well. So, according to Ericsson, that's what it takes to become really skilled. It turns out that practice really does make perfect, and in order to learn something and become very successful at doing it, all you'll need is about 10,000 hours!

Sebastian, comic book writer

Alma, chemist

Henry, saxophonist

4 LISTENING

a ● 03.02 Listen to Sebastian, Alma, and Henry talk about their learning experiences. Answer the questions.

1 Who talks about … ?
  a the best time to learn
  b learning hours
  c the strength of memory

2 Do the speakers think the learning ideas they talk about work for them?

b ● 03.02 Listen again and take notes about the things they talk about.

1 Sebastian
  a copying comics
  b friends
  c graphic design

2 Alma
  a chemistry
  b system for remembering symbols
  c colleagues' attitudes

3 Henry
  a tour preparation
  b daily learning routine
  c results

c 💬🗨 Whose ideas do you think make more sense? Why?

5 GRAMMAR Multi-word verbs

a What is the meaning of the multi-word verbs in **bold**? Which multi-word verb is most similar to the verb on its own?

1 All of my friends **were** also really **into** comic books, but none of them tried to **come up with** their own stories.

2 … so we decided to **try** it **out**

b ≫ Now go to Grammar Focus 3A on p. 138.

6 SPEAKING

a Think of something you've done that you have put a lot of effort into. For example:

- your job
- a free-time activity
- study of some kind
- playing a musical instrument
- learning a language.

Take notes about these questions:
1 What special skills or talent do you need?
2 What level of ability do you think you have achieved?
3 How have you learned new information necessary for this activity?
4 Do you need to remember a lot of things to do this well?
5 How much time have you put into it?

b 💬🗨 Work in small groups. Tell each other about your activity. Ask questions.

c 💬🗨 Who in your group do you think has put in the most effort? Who has been successful?

3B | THERE ARE A LOT OF GOOD RUNNERS IN KENYA

Learn to discuss sports activities and issues

G Present perfect and present perfect continuous

V Words connected with sports

1 READING

a Look at the photos. What sports do they show?

b 💬 What do you think makes a successful athlete or sportsperson? Choose the five things in the box you think are the most important. Are there any you think are unimportant?

> attitude   general level of fitness   luck
> desire for money   genetic makeup
> support from the community   technique
> parents   training and practice

c 💬 Compare your ideas with other students.

d Read the text "Born to Be the Best" about professionals in four sports. In what way are they all similar?

e Read the text again and answer the questions about each sport.
   1 What sport is it?
   2 Who is given as an example?
   3 What unusual features are mentioned?
   4 What is the result?

f Which of the things in 1b are mentioned in the text? Do you think this is important for all sports activities or only for top professional players?

Born to Be THE·BEST

CHAMPION SKIER

Champion cross-country skier Eero Mäntyranta had an unusual gene which made him produce too many red blood cells. Cross-country skiers cover long distances, and their red blood cells have to send oxygen to their muscles. Mäntyranta had about 65% more red blood cells than the normal adult male, and that's why he **performed** so well. In the 1960, 1964, and 1968 Winter Olympic Games, he won a total of seven medals. In 1964, he beat his closest **competitor** in the 15-kilometer race by 40 seconds.

CENTER OF GRAVITY

When American-Croatian soccer star Christian Pulisic dribbles the ball past the **opposing** team to score a goal, people often comment that the ball seems "glued to his feet." How does he achieve this? Partly through **training** and **technique**, of course, but it also helps that he is shorter than many soccer players, and as a result has a lower center of gravity. This accounts for his ability to stay on his feet in spite of being pushed and tackled by the opposing team.

THE WORLD'S BEST RUNNERS

Why do so many of the world's best distance runners come from Kenya and Ethiopia? Because a runner needs not just to be thin, but also to have thin legs and ankles. Runners from the Kalenjin tribe, in Kenya – where most of the country's best **athletes** come from – are thin in exactly this way. Compared to Europeans, Kalenjins are shorter but have longer legs, and their lower legs are over a pound lighter.

BEST AT BASKETBALL

The average height of players in the National Basketball Association is just over two meters (compared with the national average for men of 1.76 m). But some top players are not that tall – the NBA's first three-time slam-dunk champion player Nate Robinson, for example, is only 1.75 m. So how does he play so well? Well, it turns out that although he's short, he has an arm span of 1.85, so he's taller than he looks! And he's no exception – nearly all top **professional** basketball players have an arm span far longer than the average, which makes it easier for them to catch the ball and score points.

2 VOCABULARY
Words connected with sports

a Find words in the texts that have a similar meaning to the words in *italics*.

1 Eero Mäntyranta was a cross-country *skier who often won competitions*.
2 He *did so well* because he had more red blood cells than most skiers.
3 He easily beat the closest *person competing with him*.
4 Christian Pulisic is successful because of *regular practice* and also because of the *special way he plays*.
5 The team *playing against* him find it hard to keep him from scoring goals.
6 Most of Kenya's best *sportspeople* are from the Kalenjin tribe.
7 Basketball *players who play for a living* often have a long arm span.

b ⟫ Now go to Vocabulary Focus on p. 156.

3 LISTENING

a ▶03.06 The texts in 1d are from a book called *The Sports Gene*. Listen to the first part of a show in which people discuss the book. Answer the questions.

1 What do we know about Barbara McCallum?
2 What does she think of the ideas in the book?

b ▶03.06 Answer the questions. Then listen again and check.

1 What is the main message of the book?
  a The best athletes are often genetically different from most other people.
  b There is a particular gene which makes you a good athlete.
  c Being a good athlete is mainly a question of luck.
2 Which of the following factors does Barbara say are important in Kenyans' success in running?
  a They start running at an early age.
  b Many people have long legs.
  c Children learn to run in bare feet.
  d They train for hours every day.

c ▶03.07 Listen to the second part of the show and answer the questions.

1 What do we know about Marta Flores?
2 What does she think of the ideas in the book?

d ▶03.07 💬 Listen again and discuss the questions.

1 What does Marta notice about the people she has played against?
2 What conclusion does she reach from that?
3 In what way does she say sporting events like the Olympics are "unfair"?
4 Do you agree with her conclusion? Why / Why not?

4 GRAMMAR Present perfect and present perfect continuous

a Match sentences 1–4 with the uses of the present perfect and present perfect continuous (a–d).

1 ☐ You**'ve been playing** tennis since you were a child.
2 ☐ I**'ve read** that book.
3 ☐ I**'ve been thinking** a lot about this recently.
4 ☐ I**'ve lived** in Kenya.

a to talk about a recent completed action, e.g., *I've lost my glasses.*
b to talk about an activity that started in the past and is still continuing, e.g., *We've been waiting since this morning.*
c to talk about an experience at some unspecified time in your life, e.g., *He's climbed Mount Everest.*
d to talk about a recent activity which continued for a while (and will likely continue into the future), e.g., *I've been reading a lot of good books lately.*

b ≫ Now go to Grammar Focus 3B on p. 138.

c Add a sentence using the present perfect or present perfect continuous.

1 I don't think I could play volleyball anymore. I …
I haven't played it for years.
2 She's really fit. She …
3 Of course I can play chess. I …
4 Why don't you buy a new pair of skis? You …

d Think about a sport (or other free time activity) that you have been doing for a while. Take notes about questions 1–4.

1 How long have you been doing this sport or activity? Why did you start?
2 How good are you at it?
3 What are the main reasons you have/haven't become good at it? Does it have to do with … ?
   • your genetic makeup and natural ability
   • developing technique and practicing
   • support from other people
4 Do you think any of the things you have read or heard in this lesson are relevant to the activity you've been doing?

e 💬 Tell other students about your activity.

5 READING AND SPEAKING

a Read about three famous athletes and answer the questions.

1 How are they similar?   2 How are they different?

b Think about the questions.

If "sports aren't as fair as we like to think," should players be allowed to find ways to improve their performance? Which of the following do you think are acceptable? Why?
   • training hard
   • having an operation (e.g., replacing arm muscles, improving eyesight)
   • taking legal substances to enhance their performance (e.g., energy drinks)
   • taking illegal substances to enhance their performance (e.g., drugs)

c 💬 Compare your ideas. Do you agree?

CHRIS FROOME

World class British racing cyclist Chris Froome is well known for his outstanding performance in international races, including the Tour de France, which he has won four times, and the 2016 Olympics, where he was awarded a bronze medal. Froome suffers from asthma, which is a common problem among racing cyclists. He takes drugs to control his asthma, and this caused problems when he was given a blood test after a win in 2017. The test revealed that he had twice the permitted amount of salbutamol, a drug used to treat asthma that also builds muscle and improves performance. Froome claimed he took the drug on the advice of his doctor to control a severe asthma attack, and after an investigation, the case against him was dropped.

MARIA SHARAPOVA

Because of her spectacular sports career, Russian tennis star Maria Sharapova has become a household name, known even to people who don't follow tennis. She was ranked the world's number one player five times and she has won 35 singles titles in her career, including five major international tournaments. However, her professional career has not been free of controversy. In 2016, Sharapova was banned from playing for two years after a drug test found meldonium in her blood, which can be used to improve performance. She claimed that she took the drug for health reasons and had not realized it was banned in most countries. The ruling caused a widespread public outcry, and after her appeal, the ban was reduced to 15 months. She retired from professional tennis in 2020.

MIKE WEIR

Mike Weir is one of Canada's best-known champion golfers, and he is the only Canadian player ever to win a major world championship. When he found that his eyesight was deteriorating, he decided to have laser surgery on his eyes. This restored his vision, not just to the normal 20/20 vision, but to 20/15, which is better than normal eyesight. After the operation, he went on to win a series of top golfing championships. Laser surgery is commonly used by professional golfers and tennis players and often results in "super vision," which gives them a huge competitive advantage over players with normal eyesight.

3C EVERYDAY ENGLISH
Who should we invite?

Learn to make careful suggestions
S Consonant sounds
P Keeping to the topic of the conversation

1 LISTENING

a 💬 Answer the questions.

1 Do you prefer small or big get-togethers? Why?
2 How do you prepare to have a party?

b 💬 Look at the photo of someone planning a party. What do you think this person is trying to figure out?

1 when to schedule the party
2 what music to play at the party

c ▶03.09 Listen to Part 1 and check your ideas in 1b.

d ▶03.09 Listen again. Check (✓) the topics that Martin and Lucas talk about.

how to cook nachos	Alexis' problems at work
dinner	how many people to invite
who will cook	when to have a party

e ▶03.09 Listen again. What do they say about the topics?

f ▶03.10 Listen to Part 2. What does Martin want to know about the guests?

g ▶03.10 Listen to Part 2 again and answer the questions.

1 Who seems more focused on the party plans? Why do you think so?

2 CONVERSATION SKILLS Keeping to the topic of the conversation

a Read this conversation from Part 2. How does Martin return to the original topic of the conversation? Underline the expression he uses.

LUCAS Oh, yeah, I guess. Uh, how does it sound if we don't sit down to eat?

MARTIN Lucas, we're having a dinner party. Of course we're going to sit down to eat. So, to get back to the food, I'm happy to cook for eight people …

LUCAS Hmm, I wonder what Alexis eats …

MARTIN Just let me know.

b Connect words from A and B to make expressions.

A	B
as I	were saying …
to go / get	back to …
just	was saying …
as we	getting / going back to …

c We can put two of these words before the expressions in 2b. Which words are they?

so	actually	oh	anyway

d 💬 Work in pairs. Have short conversations. You need to agree on an English language study plan and organize what to study, how much to study, when, etc.

Student A: Explain your ideas for your study plans. Make sure you keep to the topic of the conversation.

Student B: Answer your partner's questions about the study plans, but keep trying to change the topic of conversation to something else.

Switch roles.

> I think we should start with vocabulary.

> Why don't we go to the café first?

> As I was saying, we should start with …

3 PRONUNCIATION
Sound and spelling: Consonant sounds

a Look at the examples from Parts 1 and 2. Underline words that begin with the sounds in the box.

/b/ /f/ /g/ /k/ /p/ /v/

1 … it's a good idea to have a big party.
2 … if the people you invite are vegetarian or anything.
3 … cook a huge amount of food.
4 So, to get back to the guests …

b ▶03.11 Listen to these two words. Which begins with a voiced sound? Which begins with an unvoiced sound?

better   people

Do you use your lips differently in the /b/ and /p/ sounds?

c ▶03.12 Listen to six words. Which word do you hear in each pair?

1	bill	3	van	5	lap
	pill		fan		lab
2	goat	4	leave	6	bag
	coat		leaf		back

d 💬 Work in pairs. Take turns saying one word from each pair. Which word does your partner say?

4 LISTENING

a ▶03.13 Listen to Part 3. What is the main topic of Lucas and Martin's conversation?

1 food for the party   3 the guests they'll invite
2 Lucas' sister

b ▶03.13 Listen again. What do they say about the topics below? Take notes.

1 Martin's friend Bill   3 Jason, the DJ
2 dinner   4 Alexis

5 USEFUL LANGUAGE
Making careful suggestions

a Martin and Lucas make careful suggestions to each other. Can you remember the missing words?

LUCAS Don't you agree that it'd _____ _____ not to cook so much?
MARTIN We _____ _____ invite more people to meet us there.

▶03.14 Listen and check.

b Why do Martin and Lucas make careful suggestions? Choose the best answer.
1 They feel the subject matter is a little sensitive and they don't want to offend each other.
2 The party won't happen for a long time, so it doesn't feel real to them.

c Look at these examples of careful suggestions. Match the examples to the correct uses below.
a Don't you think it's a good idea to … ?
b How does it sound if we/I … ?
c Another idea might be to …
d I think maybe we should …
e I thought maybe we could …

1 Putting forward an idea carefully
2 Asking the other person to give their point of view

d Correct the careful suggestions.
1 Another idea might to be booking a DJ for the party.
2 Don't you think a good idea to invite more people?
3 Maybe I thought we could have the party outside.
4 How does it sound we only have a small cake?

e ≫ **Communication 3C** Student A: Go to p. 128. Student B: Go to p. 129.

6 SPEAKING

a You are going to have a class party. Work alone and think of ideas for the party.

- when   - party theme and music
- where   - food and drinks

b 💬 Discuss your ideas and make careful suggestions. Make sure everyone keeps to the topic of the conversation.

> We could always do it at school.

> Another idea might be to rent a space.

✓ UNIT PROGRESS TEST

→ **CHECK YOUR PROGRESS**

You can now do the Unit Progress Test.

3D SKILLS FOR WRITING
It doesn't matter what sport people choose

1 SPEAKING AND LISTENING

a 💬 Discuss the questions.

1 What's the most unusual sport you've seen or heard of? Have you ever tried it?
2 What do you think are the most popular sports in your country to participate in? Why do you think they are popular?
3 How do you think new sports become popular?

b Look at photos 1–3. What are the names of the sports? Which of these sports have you tried? Which would you like to try?

c ▶ 03.15 Marco talks to three people at a sports complex: Lizzie, Barry, and Patricia. Listen and match the speakers to the sports in the photos.

d ▶ 03.15 Listen again and take notes about each speaker:

1 reasons for choosing their sport
2 how long practicing the sport
3 future plans.

e 💬 Are any of these sports popular in your city? Why / Why not?

2 READING

a Look at the chart. Are the sentences true or false?

1 The data only shows information about the different kinds of programs members do.
2 The data doesn't give information about age or gender of members.
3 The data shows changes that happen every second year.
4 The most growth in participation is in gym training.

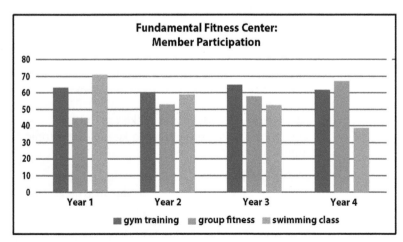

Fundamental Fitness Center: Member Participation

- gym training - group fitness - swimming class

b Read the article "Fitness: Seattle Snapshot." Does it give the same information as the chart?

c Read the article again and answer the questions.

1 What's the difference between the sports people like watching and those they like doing?
2 What was a big attraction for members when the gym first opened?
3 Why were fewer people swimming by the fourth year?
4 In which program has participation not changed a lot? Why?
5 Why was participation in group fitness classes low to begin with?
6 Why have they been so successful?

3 WRITING SKILLS
Describing data

a Look at paragraphs c, d, and e. How are they organized? Number the parts 1 to 3:

☐ a reason for the change in percentages
☐ a description of the activity
☐ a report on important increases/decreases.

b Look at paragraphs c, d, and e again and complete the chart.

	Adjective	Noun
there is a / an	[1] _____ / dramatic	increase
	obvious / significant	[2] _____
	[3] _____ / [4] _____	decrease
	Verb	**Adverb**
the number(s) / size	has/have / hasn't/ haven't increased	[5] _____ / [6] _____ / slightly
	has/have [7] _____	dramatically

c Which adjectives and adverbs describe … ?

1 a big change
2 a small change
3 a sudden change
4 a slow change
5 an important change
6 a change you can see clearly

d Answer the questions.

1 What verb phrase in paragraph d shows that there has been no change to member participation?
2 Does the <u>underlined</u> *this* in paragraphs c and d refer back or forward to other information in the paragraphs?

e Use the data about use of equipment when people work out in the gym to write sentences. Use language from 3b.

1 Members who use free weights: year 1 = 43%; year 4 = 46%
2 Members who use cardio machines: year 1 = 64%; year 4 = 41%
3 Members who use weight machines: year 1 = 48%; year 4 = 57%

4 WRITING

a Look at the chart and read the notes below. What does the information show?

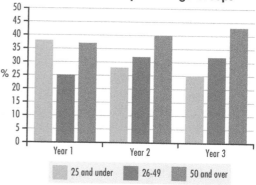

Fundamental Fitness Center Member Participation: Age Groups

Legend: 25 and under | 26-49 | 50 and over

Notes

Ages 25 and under: change gyms often – like to try something new

Ages 26-49: many have families and less time for fitness

Ages 50 and over: getting older, free of responsibility – more time for fitness

b Work in pairs. Plan an article about the data and notes in 4a. Then write your article.

c Switch your article with another pair. Does the article use language from 3b correctly? Does it include verbs and nouns? Does it have the same organization as 3a? Was it easy to understand?

FITNESS: SEATTLE SNAPSHOT

[a] Surveys show that people in Seattle love watching team sports like basketball, baseball, and soccer, but if they want to get moving, they need to do activities that don't involve watching other people chasing a ball around a field or court. Activities can include workouts at a gym, swimming, and group fitness classes. Below is an example of participation in different fitness programs at a gym in Seattle.

[b] The Fundamental Fitness Center (FFC) opened four years ago. We have group fitness classes, and our aquatic center offers a range of swimming lessons.

[c] A lot of our members do more than one activity each week, so overall, our participation rates are very high. To begin with, our swim program had the highest participation of our programs. After the first two years, there was a gradual decrease in the number of members using the pool because it was crowded at peak times. Last year, participation decreased dramatically. **This** was because a new fitness center opened nearby with an Olympic-sized pool, so a lot of members moved there.

[d] FFC also has an excellent range of machines for cardio and building strength. Participation in members' individual gym programs has remained steady over the four-year period. There was a slight decrease after the first year, and then a noticeable increase in our third year. However, participation hasn't increased or dropped below 60%. **This** is the result of a stable group of members who enjoy their workouts on a regular basis.

[e] The real success story of FFC has been our group classes, which offer a lot of variety. To begin with, a lot of members thought group workouts were just dance classes. But there has been an obvious boost in participation in group fitness over the four-year period, and last year was the most popular year for our members. Word is getting out that this is a great way to get fit – and have fun. Just recently, we've added yoga to the schedule, and numbers in those classes have increased noticeably. The reason for all of this is that we're lucky to have some really creative and motivating instructors who have helped establish these classes for our members.

[f] FFC offers a range of activities, so there is something for everyone. Also, many activities don't require as high a level of expertise as team sports do. However, it is interesting that the group classes have become increasingly popular. While people may not always like joining teams, they seem to benefit from working out in a group.

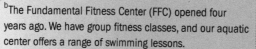

UNIT 3
Review and extension

1 GRAMMAR

a Put the words in *italics* in the correct order.

1 I didn't know Spanish before I went to Mexico, but I managed to *up / pick / it* very quickly.
2 I'm just as good as you. There's no need to *me / down / look / on* just because I didn't go to college.
3 It's still raining. This weather is starting to *get / down / me*.
4 I don't believe she was ever married to a movie star. I think she *it / up / making / is*.
5 She's very creative. She keeps *up / with / coming* new ideas.
6 I don't know how to do this task. I just can't *out / figure / it*.

b Choose the correct verb tenses in the conversations.

1 **A** Come in. Sorry the apartment is such a mess.
 B What have you ¹*done / been doing*? There are things all over the floor.
 A I've ²*cleaned / been cleaning* things out, but I haven't ³*finished / been finishing* yet.
2 **A** How are things? I haven't ⁴*seen / been seeing* you for so long. What have you ⁵*done / been doing*?
 B Oh, nothing much. I have exams coming up next month, so I've ⁶*studied / been studying* most of the time.

c Think of things you could say to answer these questions using the present perfect or present perfect continuous.

- What have you been doing these days?
- How's your family?
- You're looking fit. Have you been exercising a lot?
- So what's new?

d 💬 Have conversations, starting with the questions in 1c.

2 VOCABULARY

a Rewrite the sentences, using the word in parentheses, so that they keep the same meaning. More than one answer is possible.

1 We're looking for someone who can lead a team of researchers. (ability)
2 She can design things very well. (skilled)
3 The members of the band all play music extremely well. (outstanding)
4 He could become a very good politician. (potential)
5 He's better than most goalkeepers. (exceptional)
6 My sister can cook very well. (extraordinary)

b Give a different form of the words in *italics* to complete the definitions.

1 Someone who *coaches* athletes is a ___coach___ .
2 A person who *competes* in a sport is a _____ .
3 *Athletes* are usually very fit and _____ .
4 Someone who plays sports as a *profession* is a _____ sportsperson.
5 If you *perform* well, you give a good _____ .
6 A team that wins a *victory* is _____ .

3 WORDPOWER *up*

a Match the comments with the pictures.

1 ☐ "**Drink up**. We need to go."
2 ☐ "Could you **speak up**? We can't hear you."
3 ☐ "I **used up** the shampoo. Is there any more?"
4 ☐ "Let me see the bill. I think they've **added** it **up** incorrect[ly]"

b Adding *up* often gives an extra meaning to a verb. In which examples in 3a does *up* mean … ?

a to the end   b together   c louder

c What does *it* mean in each example below?

a suggestion   a language   a glass   a word

1 You dropped it, so I think you should **clean** it **up**.
2 I don't know. I'll have to **look** it **up**.
3 It was easy. I **picked** it **up** in about six months.
4 Why don't you **bring** it **up** at the meeting?

d ▶ 03.16 Listen and check your answers. What was th[e] problem in each case?

e Here are some more multi-word verbs with *up*. Match the two parts of the sentences.

1 Walk more slowly! I can't   **look up to** him.
2 He's a good father. His children really   **turned up**.
3 We invited 50 people, but only a few   **put up with** him[.]
4 He's so rude. I don't know why people   **keep up with** yo[u]

f Match the multi-word verbs in 3e with these meaning[s].

a tolerate   c appear or arrive
b go at the same speed   d admire or respect

g 💬 Work in pairs. Choose two of the multi-word verb[s] in 3a, c, or e. Think of a situation and write a short conversation which includes both verbs.

h 💬 Act out your conversation. Can other students guess your situation?

⟳ REVIEW YOUR PROGRESS

How well did you do in this unit? Write 3, 2, or 1 for each objective.
3 = very well   2 = well   1 = not so well

I CAN …	
discuss ability and achievement	☐
discuss sports activities and issues	☐
make careful suggestions	☐
write a description of data.	☐

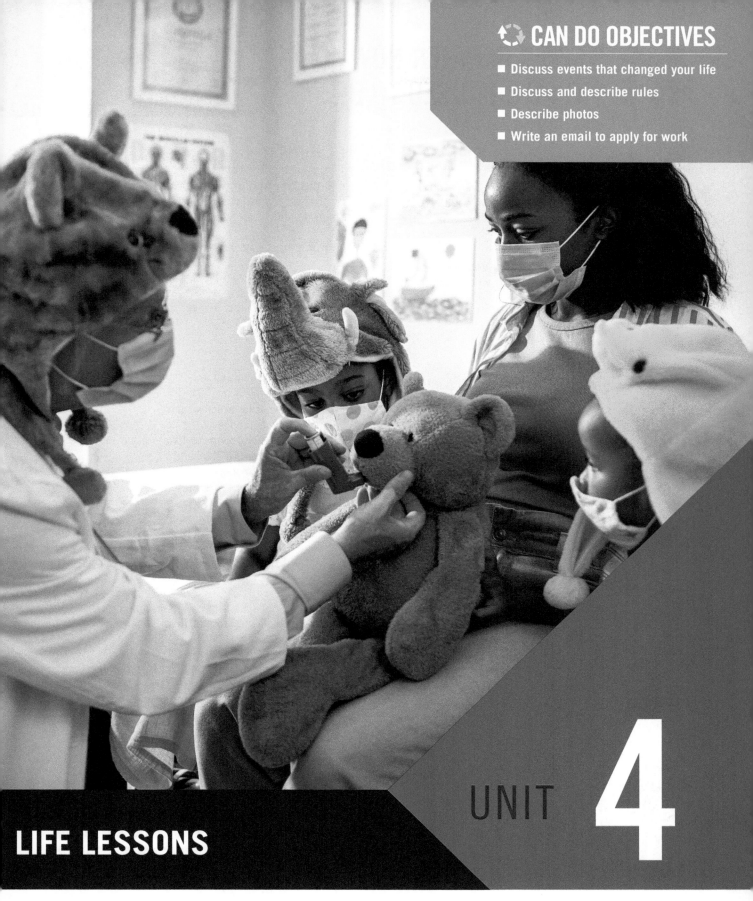

CAN DO OBJECTIVES

- Discuss events that changed your life
- Discuss and describe rules
- Describe photos
- Write an email to apply for work

UNIT 4

LIFE LESSONS

GETTING STARTED

a 💬🗨 Look at the picture and answer the questions.

1. Where are these people? What are they doing?
2. What is the doctor showing the children? Why?
3. What do you think the children are thinking?

b 💬🗨 Discuss the questions.

1. Is it important to help children prepare for what might happen to them later in life? Why?
2. Which of your childhood experiences have had an impact on your adult life?
3. In general, how much do you think experiences in childhood influence the choices you make in your life?

4A | SHE'S HAPPIER NOW THAN SHE USED TO BE

Learn to discuss events that changed your life

G *used to* and *would*
V Cause and result

1 SPEAKING

a 💬 Imagine you suddenly became very rich, either by winning or inheriting money. How would you spend the money if you had … ?

   a $10,000   b $100,000   c $1,000,000

b 💬 Do you know anyone (either someone you met or someone you read about) who has won or inherited money? What did they do with the money?

2 READING

a Read the first part of two news stories about people who won the lottery. What do you think the people did? Which person do you think spent the money most wisely?

b The words in the boxes are keywords from each story.

Sharon Tirabassi:
lottery ticket   lifestyle   extravagant   a fortune   generous   modest   family photos   regret   children   bank account

Ihsan Khan:
taxi driver   dream   number   luxuries   hometown   election   mayor   earthquake   school   satisfied

Find words in the boxes which mean:
1 a huge amount of money
2 process of choosing someone for a position
3 a sudden movement of the earth
4 spending a lot of money
5 giving a lot to other people
6 pleased you have what you want
7 the leader of the city government
8 small and not expensive.

c 💬 What do you think happened to each lottery winner?

d ≫ **Communication 4A** Student A: Read the story of Sharon Tirabassi on p. 127 and answer the questions.
Student B: Read the story of Ihsan Khan on p. 128 and answer the questions.

e 💬 Work in the same pairs. Take turns telling your stories and include the keywords in 2b. Ask questions about your partner's story to check anything you don't understand.

How to spend a
$10 MILLION LOTTERY WIN
in less than three years

Fifteen years ago, Sharon Tirabassi won $10.5 million in the lottery, but you wouldn't know it if you met her now. She lives in a rented house, she works part time as a cleaner, and she doesn't even own a car.

LOTTO WINNER TAKES HOME FORTUNE to PAKISTAN

People who win the lottery usually spend their money on things they've always wanted: a dream vacation or a beautiful house. But Ihsan Khan had a different idea. He kept his money and brought it back to Battagram, the town in Pakistan where he grew up.

f  Discuss the questions.

1 What wise decisions do you think Sharon and Ihsan made? What unwise decisions did they make?
2 Why do you think they made these decisions?
3 Which moral or "message" comes out of these stories for you? Write it down and compare your idea with other students.

> **Be careful what you wish for!**

> **Believe in your dreams.**

> **If you have a lot of money, spend it wisely!**

3 GRAMMAR *used to* and *would*

a Look at sentences a–c and complete the rules with the words in the box.

a Ihsan Khan **used to** work as a taxi driver and security guard in the U.S.
b He **used to** think he could use his money to fix everything.
c She **would** go on extravagant vacations in the Caribbean.

> now   past   used to (x2)   would (x2)

> We use *used to* and *would* to talk about things in the ¹_____ that are no longer true ²_____.
> To talk about states, thoughts, and feelings in the past, we can only use ³_____, not ⁴_____.
> To talk about habits and repeated actions, we can use either ⁵_____ or ⁶_____.

b Look again at the text about Sharon Tirabassi on p. 127. Find and <u>underline</u> other examples of *used to* and *would*.

c Look at the sentences and answer the questions.

a She **doesn't** live in a huge house **anymore**.
b He used to think he could use his money to fix everything, but he **no longer** believes that.

1 What do the words in **bold** mean?
(a) things are the same as before
(b) things are different now

2 Rewrite sentence a with *no longer* and sentence b with *not anymore*. How does the word order change?

d ≫ Now go to Grammar Focus 4A on p. 140.

e Express these ideas in a different way, using expressions from 2a–c. Try to think of two ways to say the same idea.

1 Money isn't important to me, but it was before.
   Money used to be very important to me.
   Money isn't important to me anymore.
2 When I was younger, I went shopping for clothes every Saturday, but not now.
3 I eat healthier food now.
4 I don't go out much these days. I usually stay at home.

4 LISTENING

a You are going to listen to an interview with Monica Sharpe, a researcher in the psychology of money. How do you think she will answer these questions?

1 Does winning a lot of money make you behave badly?
2 Does having a lot of money make you happy?
3 Does buying things make you happy?

b ▶04.04 Listen and check your answers.

c ▶04.04 Check (✓) the points Monica makes. Listen again and check.

1 ☐ Most people who get a lot of money spend it all quickly.
2 ☐ We enjoy hearing stories about people who won the lottery and then lost all their money.
3 ☐ Suddenly having a lot of money usually has a negative effect on you.
4 ☐ Most people feel much happier just after they win money.
5 ☐ In the long term, being rich doesn't always make you happier.
6 ☐ It's better to spend money on things you can own, like houses and cars.

d  Which of the points in 4c do you agree with? Can you think of examples from people you know or have heard about?

5 VOCABULARY Cause and result

a ▶04.05 <u>Underline</u> the correct words in **bold**. Then listen and check your answers.

1 Of course people like to believe that winning money leads **into** / **to** disaster.
2 The idea that winning a lot of money **causes** / **is caused by** misery is actually a myth.
3 Suddenly having a lot of money is just as likely to have a positive effect **on** / **to** you as a negative effect.
4 They measured how happy people are as a result **from** / **of** winning the lottery.
5 Getting richer doesn't actually **effect** / **affect** how happy you are.
6 But spending money on experiences usually results **in** / **on** longer-term happiness.

b Answer the questions about the expressions in 5a.

1 Which expressions have a similar meaning to "causes"?
2 Which expression has a similar meaning to "caused by"?
3 What is the difference between *affect* and *effect*?
4 Look at sentences 4 and 6. In which sentence is *result* a verb and in which is it a noun?

c Complete the sentences with the words in the box.

affect   effect   cause   lead   result (x2)

1 He's much friendlier than he used to be. Getting married has had a positive _____ on him.
2 Having no money at all can often _____ to problems in a relationship.
3 I hear John and Barbara have split up. I hope it won't _____ our friendship with them.
4 It's well known that smoking can _____ cancer.
5 Hundreds of villagers' lives were saved as a _____ of Ihsan Khan's help.
6 Be careful! Borrowing large amounts of money can _____ in serious financial problems.

d Think about an important event in your own life and another event that happened as a result. Write three sentences about it using expressions in 5a.

e 💬 Read your sentences to each other and ask questions.

6 LISTENING

a Look at the information about Alfonso and Dragana. How do you think their lives have changed? Think about:

lifestyle   attitude to life   daily routine   work   money   leisure

LIFE-CHANGING EVENTS

Sometimes a single big event can change your life. Two people tell us their stories.

Dragana studied abroad for a year.

Alfonso and Carmen just had their first baby.

b ▶04.06 Listen to Alfonso and Dragana. Which of the topics in 6a do they talk about?

c ▶04.06 Are the sentences true or false? Correct the false sentences. Listen again and check.

Alfonso
1 They both used to work.
2 They didn't have much money.
3 The baby hasn't changed his attitude to life much.

Dragana
4 She's from a big city in Croatia.
5 She didn't enjoy being in Berlin.
6 The experience has changed her attitude to other cultures.

7 SPEAKING

a Think about yourself now and how you have changed in the last ten years. Take notes on some of these topics:

● work
● free time
● attitude to life
● daily routine
● family and relationships
● money

b 💬 Tell each other how you think you have changed using *used to* / *would*.

4B WE WEREN'T ALLOWED TO TALK IN CLASS

1 SPEAKING

a 💬 Look at photos a–d. Which of the jobs would you most like to do? Why?

b Read what these people say about training. Do you agree with their opinions?

2 GRAMMAR Modality review

a <u>Underline</u> all the modal verbs or phrases (e.g., *can*, *have to*) in the quotes.

b Complete the rules with the correct modal verb or phrase in 2a.

1 We use _____, _____, and _____ when we talk about something that's necessary.
2 We use _____ to talk about something that isn't necessary.
3 We use _____ when we talk about something that's possible.
4 We use _____ to talk about something that's not possible.

> You can do all the studying you like, but until you've done the actual job, you don't know what it really involves.
>
> **Sheela,**
> pilot

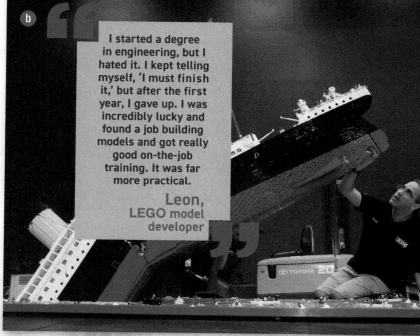

> I started a degree in engineering, but I hated it. I kept telling myself, 'I must finish it,' but after the first year, I gave up. I was incredibly lucky and found a job building models and got really good on-the-job training. It was far more practical.
>
> **Leon,**
> LEGO model developer

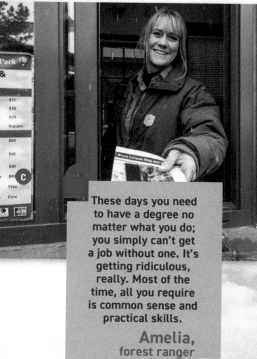

> These days you need to have a degree no matter what you do; you simply can't get a job without one. It's getting ridiculous, really. Most of the time, all you require is common sense and practical skills.
>
> **Amelia,**
> forest ranger

> You don't have to have a college degree to get a good job these days – it's as much about training and practice.
>
> **Tony,**
> stuntman

3 READING

a 💬🔊 Look at photos a–d and answer the questions.
1 What jobs are shown in the photos?
2 What kind of training do you need for this work?

b Read the texts. Were your ideas correct?

c Read the texts again. Who do you think would say this: Joe (J), Amelia (A), or both (B)?
1 There are some situations I can never really prepare for.
2 I couldn't rush things with the training program.
3 I really needed the strength I developed doing workouts at the gym.
4 It's good to have a certification, but I learned most things just by doing them.
5 Sometimes when I get home, I just feel exhausted.
6 I need to take care not only of myself but also the other members of the team.
7 I try not to let my feelings show.
8 I never stop training and learning.

d 💬🔊 Which of the two kinds of training seems harder to you? Which one would you choose to do? Why?

4 VOCABULARY Talking about difficulty

a These are definitions of the **bold** adjectives in the text. Notice the differences in meaning. Which word in bold is not as strong as the others?
1 very difficult because the training is thorough and detailed
2 difficult because you need a lot of effort and energy
3 hard because you need to give it a lot of time and attention
4 difficult and extremely tiring
5 involves hard physical work that makes your body sore
6 extremely tiring and difficult – you need a lot of effort and determination
7 difficult to deal with and needs careful attention or skill
8 difficult to deal with or do – you need to be physically and emotionally strong
9 difficult because there are rules that must be obeyed
10 so difficult you have to push yourself almost to the point of hurting yourself

Training for the
EMERGENCY FRONT LINE

Training to Rescue

You go for an easy hike in the mountains. Suddenly the weather changes and you lose sight of the trail. What should you do? Call for help and wait for Joe Conte to appear.

Joe is a Mountain Search and Rescue volunteer who risks his life to save people who get into trouble in the wilderness. Based in Colorado, Joe is a computer programmer by day. But his real passion is anything to do with mountains. Joe is one of the most experienced volunteers and often undertakes extremely dangerous rescue missions.

Can anyone become a volunteer? "Well, we welcome anyone who wants to get involved," said Joe, "but if you want to do serious rescues, you must undergo a ¹**rigorous** training program."

To begin with, you have to be an experienced mountaineer, and you have to be fit. "On rescue missions, you often face ²**arduous** conditions, so you need strength and ability," Joe pointed out.

The training takes two years and is ³**demanding** and ⁴**exhausting**. "In one training scenario, you have to rescue someone from a gap between rocks. You have to pull them up by a rope, so you need to be really strong. In another scenario, you dig someone out of an avalanche. It's ⁵**backbreaking** work, and you have to be fast because victims can only survive for about 40 minutes buried in snow."

Apart from the ⁶**grueling** physical training, volunteers need expert risk assessment skills. They often find themselves in ⁷**tricky** situations where not only the lives of the victims are in danger but also those of volunteers. "You have to make good decisions, and you have to make them quickly."

And the training never stops. Fully trained volunteers still do about 300 hours of ongoing training every year.

"Yeah, it's a big commitment, but the reward of bringing someone to safety makes it worth it."

Training to Save Lives

Being a nurse is demanding, but some nurses want an even bigger challenge and move into emergency room (ER) nursing. The ER is fast-paced and often chaotic, so ER nurses not only need to be patient and understanding, but they must also know how to multitask and stay calm under pressure.

Amelia Davis has been an ER nurse for the past six years at one of the busiest hospitals in California. She is the first point of contact for patients who arrive at the ER. Many have life-threatening medical conditions, such as heart attacks. Amelia has to know exactly what to do before a doctor can see the patient.

How do you train for such a ⁸**tough**, high-stress job? "In some ways, you don't!" was Amelia's surprising answer. "Obviously, you have to be a fully trained nurse, but I didn't do separate training to work in the ER."

Amelia passed a test for ER nurses, which gave her an official certificate. However, the certification is optional – it isn't required to work as an ER nurse.

"My training was on the job, and the discipline was ⁹**strict**," Amelia explained.

b Answer the questions about the differences in meaning.

1 You can describe training as *arduous* or *grueling*. Which has a stronger meaning?
2 Environmental conditions can be *tough* or *arduous*. Which has a stronger meaning?
3 Work can be *demanding*, *exhausting*, or *backbreaking*. Which adjective means it makes you tired? Which means it challenges you physically? Which means it can be both a physical and an emotional challenge?
4 A situation can be *tough* or *tricky*. Which adjective suggests the situation is difficult and complicated?
5 Pace can be *demanding* or *punishing*. Which has a stronger meaning?
6 Discipline can be *tough* or *strict*. Which adjective gives a stronger idea of being careful about following rules?

c Ask and answer the questions. Give extra details.

1 What is something tough you have done?
2 Can you remember a teacher you had at school who was very strict?
3 What's a job that requires rigorous training?
4 Have you ever been in a tricky situation? What happened?

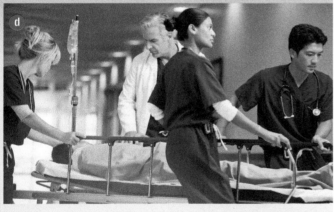

"When I first started, the head nurse was hard on the inexperienced nurses, but she knew what she was doing. I really respected her, and she prepared us for dealing with all kinds of situations."

ER nurses never know who's going to show up, so they must be ready for anything. Also, they never know when patients are going to arrive, and there are times when the ER gets unbelievably busy.

"At the beginning, I found the pace ¹⁰**punishing**. In my first week, there was a bus crash with a lot of injured people. One of the passengers was pregnant and in pain. I had the feeling she was in labor and not injured, so I called a doctor quickly. Sure enough, the baby was about to arrive. It was a complicated birth, and the doctor told me it was good I called him as soon as I did. Despite all the training, you also have to trust your instincts."

A key part of Amelia's on-the-job training was not letting her emotions get in the way. An ER nurse needs to keep a clear head at all times.

"Even after six years, some days are really hard and stressful. But it's never boring and you do save lives. That's why I'm a nurse."

d Now go to Vocabulary Focus 4B on p. 157.

5 LISTENING

a 04.09 Listen to Miranda, who trained at a drama school, and Fred, who trained at a soccer academy. Which sentence describes their experience best?

1 They both enjoyed the training but felt they missed a part of growing up.
2 They weren't sure about the training, but they know they'll do well anyway.
3 They weren't sure about the selection process, but they feel they did well during the training.

b 04.09 Listen again. Are the sentences true or false?

Miranda

1 During the audition process, she had to perform scenes from plays twice.
2 She was confident she would get into drama school.
3 All her tutors were tough.
4 The school was flexible when she wasn't sure if she wanted to continue training.

Fred

5 His parents were unsure whether he should join the academy.
6 They knew they would have to sacrifice a lot of time to help Fred.
7 He was surprised to find that he enjoyed analyzing soccer games.
8 He felt disappointed for his friend, Jack.

c Do you think the kind of sacrifice that Miranda and Fred made was worth it? Why / Why not?

6 GRAMMAR
Obligation and permission

a Look at the words and phrases in **bold** in sentences 1–6. Which show obligation (O) and which show permission (P)?

1 I **was supposed to** prepare a song as well, but they forgot to let me know.
2 … there was a workshop for a day where they **made** us work on new scenes from plays …
3 … in her class we **weren't allowed to** talk or use our voices in any way.
4 … they could see this was a pretty unique opportunity, so they **let** me do it.
5 … we **were allowed to** see the games for free.
6 … there were some boys who **were forced to** give it all up …

b Now go to Grammar Focus 4B on p. 140.

7 SPEAKING

a Think of a time (at school or work or in sports or music) when you had to do some training and follow rules. Take notes about the questions.

What was the situation?
Who made the rules?
Were some of the rules very strict?
Were there some rules you didn't follow?
How did you feel about the experience?

b Discuss your experiences. What similarities and differences were there?

4C EVERYDAY ENGLISH
They're not *that* boring

Learn to describe photos
P Contrastive stress
S Expressing careful disagreement

1 LISTENING

a 💬🗨 Discuss the questions.

1 How do you feel about posting things on social media? Do you … ?
   a post selfies of you and your friends
   b post photos of interesting things, but not of yourself
   c not post anything, but look at other people's photos
2 How do you feel about people commenting and/or criticizing photos on social media?

b Look at the photo. Who do you think the people are? What are they talking about?

c ▶ 04.12 Listen to Part 1 and check your ideas.

d ▶ 04.12 Answer the questions. Listen again and check.

1 Which photos get more likes than others?
2 How many new followers did they get from one photo?
3 What's their plan for the next assignment?

2 USEFUL LANGUAGE Describing photos

a Which of the expressions below could describe the photos? Write *1*, *2*, *n* (neither), or *b* (both).

1 ☐ And here's a <u>close-up</u> of some plants by the lake.
2 ☐ We tried to get a <u>wide-angle shot</u> with this photo.
3 ☐ Here's an <u>action shot</u> of the scene.
4 ☐ And this is with a <u>filter</u> so the light isn't too bright.
5 ☐ Here's another shot of the tree, but <u>from a different angle</u>.
6 ☐ As you can see, there are mountains <u>in the background</u>.
7 ☐ Those flowers are daffodils <u>in the foreground</u>.
8 ☐ This one's a little <u>out of focus</u>!

b ▶ 04.12 Which <u>underlined</u> expression in 2a did they NOT use? Listen again and check.

c ≫ **Communication 4C** Student A: Go to p. 128. Student B: Go to p. 129.

d 💬🗨 Work in pairs (one student from A and B in each pair). Take turns showing your photos to your partner. Ask questions about your partner's photos.

e 💬🗨 Discuss the photos. In what ways are the photos similar? In what ways are they different?

3 LISTENING

a ▶ 04.13 Listen to Part 2. Answer the questions.

1 What are Jenna and Zack talking about?
2 Who will do the next photoshoot?

b Who thinks these things, Jenna (J) or Zack (Z)?

1 Action shots are exciting.
2 Photoshoots take too long.
3 He/She has some great ideas for the new products.

4 CONVERSATION SKILLS
Expressing careful disagreement

a ▶️ 04.14 Look at the exchange between Zack and Jenna. Then listen to what they actually say. What is the difference?

ZACK Yeah, action shots. So difficult.
JENNA I don't agree. They're not at all difficult.

b Why does Jenna use careful ways to disagree?

c The sentences below are replies to what another person said. What do you think each speaker is talking about? Match the replies with the topics in the box.

| a soccer game   a movie   senior economists
| a restaurant meal   a party |

1 <u>Really, do you think so? I thought</u> he played really well.
2 <u>I'm not sure about that.</u> It doesn't seem that expensive.
3 <u>I know what you mean, but on the other hand,</u> it's a very challenging job.
4 <u>Oh, I don't know.</u> I think we could have a really good time.
5 <u>Maybe you're right,</u> but I enjoyed some parts of it.

d ▶️ 04.15 Listen to the conversations and check your answers.

e 💬📱 How could you disagree with the comments below? Prepare replies using the <u>underlined</u> expressions from 4c. Then take turns replying.

1 I love Café Roma. It's a great atmosphere.
2 I'd never want to have a cat. All they do is sit around and sleep.
3 I don't know why people play golf. It's such a boring sport.

5 PRONUNCIATION Contrastive stress

a ▶️ 04.14 Listen again to Jenna's reply and answer the questions below.

ZACK Yeah, action shots. So difficult.
JENNA Oh, I don't know, **they're not that difficult**.

1 Underline the word which has the strongest stress in the **bold** sentence.
2 Does the sentence mean … ?
   a They're not all difficult.
   b They're not as difficult as you think they are.
   c They're not as difficult as other kinds of photoshoots.

b 💬📱 Reply to the comments below using *not that*.

1 I thought that was a really interesting lecture.

> Oh, I don't know. …

2 I think photography is a very difficult subject.
3 Look at that tree. It's so unusual.
4 I thought the questions on the test were incredibly easy.

c ▶️ 04.16 Listen and check. Were your replies similar?

6 LISTENING

a ▶️ 04.17 Listen to Part 3. Which of these is the best summary of what happens?

1 Jenna and Zack talk about photos she took and uploaded that he is going to edit. Zack asks Jenna to take photos of his wedding.
2 Jenna says she doesn't like editing and she's glad Zack likes to edit photos. Zack says he needs to start editing the photos.

b 💬📱 Are the sentences true or false? Discuss the false sentences – what actually happens?

1 Jenna put the best photos in a folder.
2 Jenna likes to take and edit photos.
3 Zack will choose the photos that Jenna took.
4 Zack is planning his wedding to Elizabeth.
5 Jenna can't be the wedding photographer.
6 Zack says he wants action shots and close-ups at his wedding.

7 SPEAKING

a ≫ Communication 4C Student A: Go to p. 127. Student B: Go to p. 129.

b Present an opinion on one of the topics to the rest of the class. Do they agree with you?

✓ UNIT PROGRESS TEST

→ CHECK YOUR PROGRESS

You can now do the Unit Progress Test.

4D SKILLS FOR WRITING
I'm good at communicating with people

1 SPEAKING AND LISTENING

a 💬 If you go to live in a different country, do you think it's important to … ?
- learn the local language
- make friends with local people
- go somewhere beautiful with a good climate

Why do you think these things are important or not important?

Nick from the U.S.

Katowice, Poland

Jean from France

Muscat, Oman

Eva from Colombia

Toronto, Canada

b ▶ 04.18 Listen to three people talking about living in the places in the photos. Which topics do they mention?

meeting people   the climate   food and drink
the culture of the country   speaking the language

c ▶ 04.18 Listen again. Answer these questions about each speaker.
1 What did he/she like?
2 What did he/she find difficult?
3 How was it different from his/her own country?

d Which speakers make these points? How did their own experience support these opinions?
1 It's important to learn the local language.
2 Beautiful cities aren't always the best places to live.
3 The weather influences the way people live.
4 Foreigners often don't make an effort to get to know the local culture.
5 Living abroad can be worthwhile even if you don't always have a good time.

e 💬 The speakers say that meeting local people is important when you live in a different country. Think of three ways you could meet local people. Which is your most interesting idea? Why?

2 READING

a Read the ad about becoming an international student "buddy" in Chicago. Answer the questions.
1 What is a "buddy" and what does he/she do?
2 What are the advantages of becoming a buddy?
3 What kind of person are they looking for?

Be a buddy for
THE INTERNATIONAL STUDENTS' CLUB

Are you curious about other cultures? Are you eager to get to know and meet new people from all over the world?
Volunteer to offer assistance and friendship to international students as a "buddy" at your university or college.

RESPONSIBILITIES
After an international student has been assigned to you, you will show them around during the first weeks of their stay. You'll give them insights into the student life in your area and generally help them out.

WHAT WE OFFER YOU
- free membership and benefits of belonging to the International Students' Club
- a free training class, which will look great on your résumé (a certificate of participation awarded)
- the opportunity to get a wide range of cross-cultural experiences

b Paulo wrote an email applying to be a buddy and saying why he is suitable. Which of the reasons below do you think he should use?

he understands the needs of foreign students
he loves living in Chicago
he's outgoing and sociable
he's interested in other cultures
he speaks several languages
he has plenty of free time
he knows Chicago well

Read the email and compare your answers.

3 WRITING SKILLS
Giving a positive impression

a Paulo uses phrases in his email which give a positive impression. <u>Underline</u> the phrases which have these meanings.

1 I *speak* English *well.*
2 I *like being with other people.*
3 I *have no problem talking to people.*
4 I *am able to* understand the needs of students.
5 I *know* the city *well.*
6 I have always *been interested* in learning about other countries.
7 I would be *willing* to give up some of my free time.
8 I could *help* your program.

b Paulo writes *I am sure* ... instead of *I think* ... in order to sound more confident. Find four more expressions like this in the email.

c What is the advantage of using the expressions in 3a and 3b when applying for a job? Which answer is not correct?

1 They make the writer sound positive and enthusiastic.
2 They make the email more interesting to read.
3 They give the impression that the writer could do the job well.

QUALIFICATIONS
● You're open-minded and interested in other cultures.
● You have a knowledge of English as well as other languages.

Dear International Students' Club,

[1] I saw the information about international student buddies on your website, and I am writing to apply for the role.

[2] I am a Brazilian student at the University of Chicago, where I am studying international law. I am fluent in English, Spanish, French, and Portuguese, which would help me to communicate with students from different countries. I am also very sociable and good at communicating with people, which I am sure would help me to establish a good relationship with new students.

[3] As a foreign student in Chicago myself, I am in an excellent position to understand the needs of students coming from other countries. I have a thorough knowledge of the city and the student life here. I am confident that I would be able to help students to feel at home and find their way around.

[4] I have always been eager to learn about other cultures, and my own circle of friends in Chicago is completely international. I strongly believe we should encourage people from different cultures to come together to help promote intercultural understanding.

[5] I would be more than happy to give up some of my free time to work as an international student buddy, and I'm certain I could make a valuable contribution to your program.

I look forward to hearing from you.

Best regards,
Paulo Figueiredo

4 WRITING

a Plan an email applying to do volunteer work. Choose one of these situations. Make a list of reasons why you would be suitable.

● A website is advertising for volunteers to work in an international summer camp and organize activities for teenagers.
● A volunteer organization wants helpers to make contact with English-speaking families living in your country and help them to adapt to your culture.
● A large high school in your area wants volunteers to give talks to students about different jobs and to help them decide on a future career.

b Write the email. Include:

● an opening sentence, explaining why you are writing
● two or three paragraphs, explaining why you are suitable
● phrases from 3a and 3b
● a final sentence to conclude the email.

c Work in pairs. Look at your partner's email. Does it ... ?

● make it clear why he/she is suitable
● have a clear structure
● use expressions from 3a and 3b to give a positive impression

d Switch your email with other students. Would they choose you to be a volunteer?

UNIT 4
Review and extension

1 GRAMMAR

a Use the words in parentheses to rewrite the sentences. Make sure the meaning doesn't change.

1 I was a nurse, but now I work for a drug company. (used to)
2 I don't do shift work now. (no longer)
3 When I was a nurse I sometimes slept in, but now I always get up early. (would)
4 I no longer take my lunch to work because there's a cafeteria at the drug company. (anymore)
5 I wore a uniform in my old job, but now I wear my own clothes. (used to)
6 I don't have to deal with difficult patients now. (no longer)
7 I'm much happier than I was before. (used to)

b Correct five obligation and permission expressions in the text.

I went to a very strict elementary school when I was a child. I wasn't allowed to do about two hours of homework every night, which meant there was little time to play with my friends. But often my parents told me just to study for an hour and wrote a note for the teacher excusing me from homework. In class we weren't let to talk to each other when we were working on a task because teachers didn't like noisy classrooms. However, we allowed to put up our hand and ask our teacher a question as she felt it was good to help students. We weren't allowed to do some kind of physical exercise every day after lunch, but that made us very tired in the afternoon. One good thing is that they supposed us learn a musical instrument and I learned to play the clarinet, which I still enjoy doing.

2 VOCABULARY

a Complete the sentences with a preposition followed by your own idea.

1 Tiredness is usually caused _____ …
2 A sunny day always has a positive effect _____ …
3 Too much exercise can result _____ …
4 Visiting a foreign country can lead _____ …
5 As a result _____ learning English, I …

b 💬 Work in pairs. Compare your ideas. Ask your partner why they completed the sentences in that way.

c Which word in the box collocates best with the nouns?

rigorous	tough	punishing	strict	arduous	tricky

1 _____ training program / schedule
2 _____ laws / parents
3 _____ plastic / teachers
4 _____ journey / task
5 _____ testing / training
6 _____ situation / question

d 💬 Talk about three examples in 2c that you have experienced.

3 WORDPOWER *as*

a Replace the <u>underlined</u> words with *as* expressions in the box.

as a whole   as far as restaurants are concerned
as for   as a matter of fact   as far as I'm concerned
as far as I know   as if   as follows

1 I'm glad you're happy. But <u>speaking of</u> Alan, it's impossible to please him.
2 <u>Everyone in</u> the class is improving their speaking.
3 I'm not American. <u>To tell you the truth</u>, I'm from Denmark.
4 My list of complaints is <u>below</u>: 1) There was no hot water …
5 It felt <u>like</u> we had always lived there.
6 <u>In my opinion</u>, the cost of food here is very high.
7 <u>Talking about restaurants</u>, there are some excellent ones in our neighborhood.
8 <u>From what I've seen and from what people tell me</u>, she's usually on time.

b Add a word to the blanks in 1–8 and then match to a–h.

1 [c] As far as I _____'m_____ / _____am_____
2 [ ] The key reasons for our success are as _____
3 [ ] I'm fit and well. As _____
4 [ ] As far as I _____
5 [ ] The team as _____
6 [ ] She's not boring. As _____
7 [ ] It looks as _____
8 [ ] As far as sports are _____

a … whole played very well.
b … they make the best coffee in town.
c … concerned, I go running twice a week.
d … matter of fact, she's a really interesting person.
e … my husband, he has the flu.
f … many of them are more about money than the sport.
g … 1. We trained very hard …
h … it's going to be a sunny day.

c Complete the sentences with your own ideas.

1 As far as I'm concerned, …
2 As far as I know, …
3 It looks as if …
4 Our class as a whole …
5 As far as English is concerned, …

d 💬 Tell another student your sentences and ask questions.

UNIT **5**

CHANCE

GETTING STARTED

a 💬 Look at the picture and answer the questions.

1 What is the woman doing?
2 Would you like to try something like that? Why / Why not?
3 What could the woman be thinking?
4 Imagine you're on the beach below. What would you be thinking?

b 💬 Discuss the questions.

1 Why do you think some people like doing extreme and dangerous things?
2 Do you think they do these things in spite of the risk or because of the risk?

5A | YOU COULD LIVE TO BE A HUNDRED

1 SPEAKING

Are you an OPTIMIST or a PESSIMIST?

a 💬 Are you an optimist or a pessimist? Mark your place on this scale, then compare with others in your group.

Optimist ⟷ Pessimist

b 💬 Decide what you think about the questions, then compare your answers.

1 If you take a test at the end of this class, how well will you do?

I'll get a perfect score. ⟷ I'll probably fail.

2 Do you expect the coming week to be … ?

exciting/great ⟷ boring/terrible

3 Imagine you left your bag on the bus. Do you expect to get it back?

Yes ⟷ No

4 You start a new workout routine and you're really tired the next day. Do you expect it to be easier the next time?

Yes ⟷ No

c ≫ Communication 5A Now go to p. 129.

d 💬 Based on your answers in 1b, decide who in your group … ?

- is the most optimistic
- is the most pessimistic
- is the most realistic

e Write a question to find out if other students are optimistic or pessimistic. Add a) and b) answer choices.

Example:

You want to buy a shirt you like, but the store is sold out. What do you think?

a) I'm sure I can find it somewhere else.
b) Why am I always so unlucky?

WHY WE THINK WE'RE GOING TO HAVE A LONG AND HAPPY LIFE

Researchers have found that people all over the world share an important characteristic: optimism. Sue Reynolds explains what it's all about.

WE'RE ALL ABOVE AVERAGE!

Try asking a 20-year-old these questions:

- What kind of career will you have?
- How long do you think you'll live?

Most people think they'll be able to earn above-average salaries, but only some of the population can make that much. Most young men in Europe will say they expect to live well into their 80s, but the average life expectancy for European men is 75. Most people will give an answer that is unrealistic because nearly everyone believes they will be better than the average. Obviously, they can't all be right.

Most people are also optimistic about their own strengths and abilities. Ask people, "How well do you get along with other people?" or "How intelligent are the people in your family?" and they'll usually say they're above average. Again, they can't all be right. We can't all be better than everyone else, but that's what we think.

LOOKING ON THE BRIGHT SIDE

There is a reason for this. Research has shown that, on the whole, we are optimistic by nature and have a positive view of ourselves. In fact, we are much more optimistic than realistic and frequently imagine things will turn out better than they actually do. Most people don't expect their marriages to end in divorce, they don't expect to lose their jobs, or to be diagnosed with a life-threatening disease. Furthermore, when things do go wrong, they are often quick to find something positive in all the gloom. Many people who fail exams, for example, are convinced they were just unlucky with the questions and they'll do better next time. Or people who have had a serious illness often say that it was really positive because it made them appreciate life more. We really are very good at "looking on the bright side."

Even if our optimism is unrealistic and leads us to take risks, without it we might all still be living in caves …

... we keep polluting the planet because we're sure that we'll find a way to clean it up some day ...

THE OPTIMISM BIAS

This certainty that our future is bound to be better than our past and present is known as the "Optimism Bias," and researchers have found that it is common to people all over the world and of all ages. Of course, the Optimism Bias can lead us to make some very bad decisions. Often, people don't take out travel insurance because they're sure everything will be all right, they don't worry about saving up for old age because the future looks fine, or they smoke cigarettes in spite of the health warnings on the pack because they believe "It won't happen to me." Or on a global scale, we keep polluting the planet because we're sure that we'll find a way to clean it up some day in the future.

OPTIMISM IS GOOD FOR YOU

But researchers believe that the Optimism Bias is actually good for us. People who expect the best are generally likely to be ambitious and adventurous, whereas people who expect the worst are likely to be more cautious, so optimism actually helps to make us successful. Optimists are also healthier because they feel less stress – they can relax because they think that everything is going to be just fine. Not only that, but the Optimism Bias may also have played an important part in our evolution as human beings. Because we hoped for the best, we were prepared to take risks such as hunting down dangerous animals and traveling across the sea to find new places to live, and this is why we became so successful as a species. Even if our optimism is unrealistic and leads us to take risks, without it we might all still be living in caves, too afraid to go outside and explore the world in case we get eaten by wild animals.

2 READING

a Read the article "Why We Think We're Going to Have a Long and Happy Life" quickly. Choose the correct words to complete the summary.

Most people are naturally *optimistic / pessimistic,* and this is generally *an advantage / a disadvantage* for the human race because it helps us to be *realistic about the future / more successful.*

b Read the article again. Check (✓) the five points made in the article.
1 ☐ Pessimists usually have fewer friends than optimists.
2 ☐ Humans are naturally positive about their future.
3 ☐ Reality is often worse than we imagine it to be.
4 ☐ People who live in warmer countries are usually more optimistic.
5 ☐ We often act (or don't act) because we're confident everything will work out.
6 ☐ If we imagine a better future, we will take more risks.
7 ☐ Optimists spend a lot of time daydreaming.
8 ☐ Optimism about the future makes us feel better in the present.

c Discuss the questions.
- Look again at your answers in 1b. Do you think you have the "Optimism Bias"?
- Do you agree that it's better to be optimistic than realistic? Why / Why not?
- How do you see yourself 20 years from now?

3 VOCABULARY
Adjectives describing attitude

a Find adjectives in "Why We Think We're Going to Have a Long and Happy Life" that mean:
1 expecting the future to be good
2 seeing things as they are
3 not seeing things as they are
4 prepared to take risks
5 not prepared to take risks
6 wanting to be successful.

b Which of these adjectives best describe you?

c ≫ Now go to Vocabulary Focus 5A on p. 158.

Many people who fail exams are convinced they were just unlucky with the questions ...

4 LISTENING

a Read the statistics and guess which numbers complete the sentences.

| 8,000 | 6 | 18 million | 1 million | 4 |

WHAT ARE YOUR CHANCES?

Chance of living to be 100 (man):
1 in _____

Chance of living to be 100 (woman):
1 in _____

Chance of having a car accident:
1 in _____

Chance of winning the lottery:
1 in _____

Chance of being in a plane crash:
1 in _____

b ▶05.04 Listen and check your answers. Do you think any of the statistics would be different where you live?

c ▶05.04 According to the speaker, how can you increase your chances of doing these things? Listen again and check.

1 surviving a plane crash
2 getting to the airport safely
3 living to be 100

5 GRAMMAR Future probability

a ▶05.05 Complete the sentences with the words in the box. Then listen and check.

> likely   unlikely   could   may   probably (x2)
> certainly (x2)   chance

1 It's very _____ that your plane will crash.
2 Even if it does, you'll _____ be fine because 95% of people in plane crashes survive.
3 So, if you're worried about getting on that plane, don't be, because you'll almost _____ survive the trip.
4 You're more _____ to have an accident in the car going to the airport.
5 You have a good _____ of living to be 100.
6 Modern medicine _____ make the chances higher still during your lifetime.
7 You _____ won't die in a plane crash and you _____ live to be 100.
8 But the bad news is, you almost _____ won't win the lottery.

b Which phrases in 5a mean … ?

1 it's certain / nearly certain   3 it's possible
2 it's probable   4 it's not probable

c Which words in the box in 5a are used in these patterns?

1 *will* _____ (+ verb)
2 _____ *won't* (+ verb)
3 is / are _____ to (+ verb)
4 It's _____ that …
5 There's a _____ that …

d 💬 Change these predictions, using words from 5a.

1 I'll meet someone famous in my life: 70%.
2 I'll have children: 50–60%.
3 I'll fall in love at least once in my life: 90%.
4 I'll become a millionaire: 0.05%.
5 Someone will steal from me: 80%.
6 I'll live in the same place all my life: 20%.

e ≫ Now go to Grammar Focus 5A on p. 142.

6 SPEAKING

a Do you think these things will happen in your lifetime? Decide if each event is certain, probable, possible, unlikely to happen, or if it will certainly not happen. Then add a question of your own.

1 Will we find a cure for all forms of cancer?
2 Will people go to live on Mars?
3 Will the level of the oceans continue to rise?
4 Will there be another world war?
5 Will people stop using cars?
6 Will Spanish become the world's most used language?

b 💬 Ask other students their opinion.

c 💬 Tell the class what you found out.

- How many people agreed with your opinion?
- What were the most interesting comments?
- Are people in your class generally optimistic, pessimistic, or realistic?

5B | I'LL BE SETTLING INTO MY ACCOMMODATIONS

Learn to prepare for a job interview

G Future perfect and future continuous
V The natural world

1 READING

a 💬 Look at the pictures of Antarctica and answer the questions.

1 What can you see in the pictures?
2 What do you know about Antarctica?
3 Would you like to go there? Why / Why not?

b 💬 Take the quiz. Then compare your answers with a partner.

THE UNKNOWN CONTINENT

1 HOW BIG IS ANTARCTICA?
(a) the size of Russia
(b) the size of the U.S. and Mexico
(c) the size of Australia

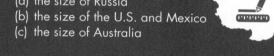

2 HOW MUCH OF ANTARCTICA IS COVERED BY ICE?
(a) 98%   (b) 86%   (c) 77%

3 WHICH OF THE FOLLOWING CAN'T YOU FIND IN ANTARCTICA?
(a) rivers   (c) trees
(b) deserts

4 WHICH OF THESE ANIMALS CAN YOU FIND THERE?
(a) polar bears
(b) seals
(c) wolves

5 WHO WAS THE FIRST PERSON TO REACH THE SOUTH POLE IN 1911?
(a) Richard Byrd (American)
(b) Robert Scott (British)
(c) Roald Amundsen (Norwegian)

c ⟫ Communication 5B Now go to p. 129.

d Read the first part of an article about working in Antarctica. What would your reaction be to a job advertisement like this?

MY LIFE ON ICE

Imagine you saw a job advertised with the following conditions:

• no leaving your place of work for six months – you must stay inside

• work six days a week, but always be available

• socialize only with your colleagues – no contact with other friends and family

You'd be crazy to apply, wouldn't you? Probably. But if you want to work in Antarctica during the winter, this is what you'll have to put up with.

e 💬 Discuss the questions.
- Why do you think people want to work in Antarctica?
- What kinds of jobs can people do there?
- What kinds of leisure activities do they do during the winter months when it's difficult to go outside?

f Read "Working in Antarctica." Does it include any of your ideas from 1e?

g Read the article again. Take notes about:
- Camilla's background
- her role at the base
- her free time
- her thoughts about Antarctica
- her colleagues at the base.

h 💬 What do you think are … ?
- the advantages of a job like Camilla's
- possible frustrations in this kind of job

Would you ever consider doing a job like this?

2 VOCABULARY The natural world

a Don't look at the article. Match words from A with words from B to make collocations.

A	B
rough	environment
environmentally	energy
solar	footprint
fragile	weather
ecological	change
global	warming
carbon	impact
climate	friendly

b Check your answers in the article.

c Complete the sentences with the collocations in 2a.
1. We're going to change our energy supply to _____ _____ to reduce our _____ _____.
2. When the steam engine was invented, not many would have thought about the _____ _____ of burning so much coal.
3. Our boat trip was canceled due to _____ _____.
4. If there is an oil spill from a ship, it will damage the _____ marine _____ in this bay.
5. Most scientists agree that irregular weather patterns are evidence of _____ _____ and _____ _____.
6. Traveling by train is slower but it's far more _____ _____ than going by plane.

Working in ANTARCTICA

When she saw an online advertisement for a Chef Manager at the United States Antarctic Program (USAP) base at McMurdo Station, chef Camilla Leal was certainly given food for thought. Camilla, in her mid-thirties, felt it was time for an adventure and a life experience that really was different.

Camilla is part of a group of key support staff at McMurdo. The main focus of USAP is scientific research into the climate, oceans, and ecosystems of Antarctica. In order to carry out this research successfully, scientists need the help of people like Camilla to make their lives as comfortable as possible.

A key responsibility for Camilla is keeping everyone happy, and one of the best ways of doing this is by keeping them well fed. This doesn't mean preparing high-end restaurant food, but it does mean organizing a lot of social events to boost the mood. However, everyone has to play their part, and Camilla makes sure no one escapes doing the dishes.

One thing that all staff at USAP share is their love of the continent. "I don't mind the rough weather," Camilla says, "and I've always found landscapes with ice and snow amazingly beautiful. Sure, I don't get to see much for six months of the year, but for the other six months there's plenty of light and the scenery is stunning." But apart from admiring the natural beauty of Antarctica, the staff all have a clear understanding of the fact that it's a fragile environment because, compared to the rest of the world, it is largely untouched. They're aware that the presence of human beings can have a significant ecological impact on the continent and, therefore, they treat it with care. USAP research stations use solar energy to heat air and hot water. "We try to be as environmentally friendly as possible," says Camilla. "We don't want to leave a carbon footprint down here."

As Camilla notes, "Antarctica can tell us a lot about what's happening in the world. It can tell us a lot about global warming and climate change. In an extreme climate like this, you really notice if things are changing."

During the winter months, all McMurdo staff try to keep themselves entertained either by making mid-winter gifts for each other or creating a murder mystery event. Camilla has also taught herself Spanish to intermediate level. However, during the summer months she goes cross-country skiing and enjoys trips to do some penguin and whale watching.

Camilla realizes that living and working in Antarctica isn't for everyone. "If you're the kind of person who likes shopping, going out for dinner, and clubbing, then forget it." She's now in her fourth year here and still finds it a unique and rewarding experience.

"I was crazy enough to apply for the job, and I've been crazy enough to stay. But it's a job that's given me so much – I've worked with some remarkable people, and I'm living in a unique and fascinating part of the world."

d Work on your own. Answer the questions and take notes.

- Are there any environments near you that are considered fragile? What kind of environments are they?
- What different human inventions have a negative ecological impact?
- What kinds of things could you do to reduce your carbon footprint?

e 💬 Discuss your answers.

3 LISTENING

a ▶ 05.08 Martha's going to Antarctica to do research on penguins. She talks to her friend Joe about her work. Listen and answer the questions.

1 How well does Joe understand Martha's research?
2 Are his questions serious or light-hearted?
3 What do we learn about the personality of the penguins?
4 Why is the research important?

b ▶ 05.08 Listen again. Number the actions in the correct order from 1 to 5.

☐ The eggs are laid.
☐ Tags are put on the penguins.
☐ Penguins find mates.
☐ Martha arrives in Antarctica.
☐ Penguin chicks are born.

4 GRAMMAR
Future perfect and future continuous

a Look at these future verb forms from the conversation in 3a and match them to the uses a–c below.

1 … this time next week **I'll be settling** into my accommodations.
2 … I think **I'll be doing** similar things every day.
3 … by the time I arrive **the penguins will already have** found mates.

a talk about an action that will be in progress at a specific time in the future
b talk about an action that will be completed before a specific time in the future
c talk about planned actions in the future

b ≫ Now go to Grammar Focus 5B on p. 142.

c Work on your own. Take notes about the questions.

- Where do you think you'll be living this time next year?
- What do you think you'll have achieved five years from now?

d 💬 Tell each other your answers to 4c and ask follow-up questions.

5 SPEAKING

a Read the job advertisement. Would you like this job?

Communications Officer in Antarctica

Responsibilities:
❄ interview researchers and collect information about their projects
❄ update our blog regularly
❄ assist all staff with IT requests

You need a friendly personality and excellent people skills.
This job is from October to March.

b Prepare a job interview role play for the job in 5a.

Student A: You want to apply for the job. Imagine you have the skills and experience that make you a suitable job applicant. Think of questions you can ask the interviewer.
Student B: You are the interviewer. Think of questions you can ask the applicant. Think of any useful information you can tell the applicant.

c 💬 Work in pairs. Do the role play.
Student A: Do you still want the job?
Student B: Do you think Student A is suitable for the job? Why / Why not?

5C EVERYDAY ENGLISH
I'm not making enough money

1 SPEAKING AND LISTENING

a 💬 Answer the questions below.

1 What are the best ways to earn money?

2 Have you ever had a roommate to help save money on rent? What are some other ways to save money?

b ▶05.11 Listen to Part 1. Put four of these events in the correct order. One event doesn't occur. Which is it?

☐ Alex asks Daniel what's wrong.

☐ Sara offers to help.

☐ Daniel asks about Jim.

☐ Sara talks about a TV show.

☐ Daniel talks about money.

c ▶05.11 Answer the questions. Listen again and check.

1 Why is Daniel worried?

2 Why is being a server a good idea?

3 What problems with being a server do they mention?

4 What does Daniel want to know about Jim?

2 LISTENING

a ▶05.12 Look at the picture of Sara, Daniel, and Alex above. Which of these topics could they be talking about? Listen to Part 2 and check.

money problems getting a roommate Alex's birthday

vacation rentals moving downtown

b ▶05.12 Listen again. Take notes about the ideas they discuss. What are the advantages and disadvantages of each idea?

3 USEFUL LANGUAGE
Discussing advantages and disadvantages

a Sara, Daniel, and Alex discuss Daniel's options for his problems. What do you think they say? Complete the sentences.

1 Of course, the _____ is, you'd have to find a roommate.

2 Yes, but the _____ is, I could keep the apartment.

b ▶05.13 Listen and check.

c Which of these words/phrases could you use in the sentences in 3a?

problem advantage disadvantage

best thing drawback

d ▶05.14 Add prepositions from the box to the expressions. Then listen and check.

of (x2) with (x2) about

one good thing _____
the advantage/disadvantage _____
the only drawback _____
another problem _____
the trouble _____

e Look at some people's ideas for the future. Use an expression from 3d in each second sentence.

1 "I might sell my car and go everywhere by bicycle. I'd be so fit."

2 "I'd love to live in Montevideo. It would be very expensive."

3 "I could work in China for a year. I don't speak the language."

4 PRONUNCIATION Intonation groups

a ▶ 05.15 Listen to these sentences. Answer the questions.

The good thing is, I could keep the apartment.
The trouble is, you'd have to find a roommate.

1 Where do you hear a slight pause?
2 Which words are stressed in the **bold** phrases?
3 Does Daniel's voice go up (↗) or down (↘) on the word *is*?

b ▶ 05.16 Listen to these sentences. Practice saying them, pausing after *is*.

1 The trouble is, I don't have enough money.
2 The point is, I still owe money to the bank.
3 The problem is, I'd need to get another job.
4 The advantage is, I'd be able to keep making art.

5 LISTENING

a ▶ 05.17 Listen to Part 3. What do they say about these things?

1 already has a room to rent
2 looking for a new job
3 needing money now
4 working at a café

b Which of these adjectives and phrases describe Alex? Which describe Daniel?

full of ideas	cautious in making decisions
enthusiastic	worried about the future

6 CONVERSATION SKILLS Responding to an idea

a Read what the speakers say. Complete the replies with the words in the box.

bad	possibility	great	worth

1 **A** I don't know, it's a big risk.
  B Not at all – I think it's a _____ idea!
2 **B** Well, how about entertainment? We could have live music and get local musicians to play on the weekend.
  A That might be _____ a try.
3 **B** Or display paintings or photos.
  A Hmm, that's not a _____ idea.
4 **B** Or readings. Have poetry readings.
  A Yeah, that's a _____.

b ▶ 05.18 Listen and check. Which of the replies is … ?

1 more enthusiastic   2 more cautious

c Look at these ways to respond to an idea. Order them from 1–6 (*1* = very cautious, *6* = very enthusiastic).

☐ It's an idea, I suppose.
☐ Yes, that makes sense.
☐ That's a great idea.
☐ What a fantastic idea!
1 Hmm, I don't know about that.
☐ Yes, good idea.

d You want to do something with the whole class at the end of the year. Write down three ideas.

We could go on a day trip.

e 💬 Work in groups. Take turns suggesting and responding to each other's ideas, using expressions in 6a and 6c. Which idea is the best?

7 SPEAKING

a ≫ Communication 5C Now go to p. 128.

b Take a class vote. Whose idea sounds the best?

✅ UNIT PROGRESS TEST

→ **CHECK YOUR PROGRESS**

You can now do the Unit Progress Test.

5D | SKILLS FOR WRITING
We need to change the way we live

Learn to write an argument for and against an idea

W Arguing for and against an idea

1 SPEAKING AND LISTENING

a 💬🎤 Discuss the questions.

1 What environmental problems are shown in photos a–d?
2 What environmental problems exist in your country or region? Which do you think are the most serious?
3 What action can people take to help solve them?

b ▶05.19 Listen to the news reports and match them with photos a–d. What key words helped you decide?

c ▶05.19 💬🎤 What did the news reports say about these topics?

1 beekeepers – bees – pesticides – farmers – fruit trees
2 air pollution – smog – masks – coal – exhaust fumes
3 plastic – birds, sea animals, and fish – the sea – 2050
4 fires – rainforest – wildfires – clearing forest for land – soccer fields

Retell the reports. Listen again if necessary.

d 💬🎤 Discuss the questions.

1 Have you ever heard a news report like those in 1b about your own country or a country you know? What happened?
2 Which of these statements do you agree with the most and why?
   • We are responsible as individuals for protecting the environment. We can solve most environmental problems by behaving in a more responsible way.
   • The main responsibility for protecting the environment should lie with governments and large companies. There isn't much that individuals can do to change things.
3 What actions do you think (a) governments, (b) large companies, and (c) individuals can take to protect the environment?

How can we help protect the environment?

Leon

[1] Modern technology has many benefits – we can produce food cheaper and in greater quantities, we can manufacture the things we need more efficiently, and we can travel and communicate more easily. On the other hand, our activities can have negative impacts on the environment. It is well known that we are polluting our oceans with plastic and chemicals, many species are dying out, and natural areas are disappearing as cities spread. Scientists agree that we need to take urgent action to protect the world we live in before it's too late. But how can we do this?

[2] Most people accept that in order to protect the environment, we need to change the way we live. As individuals, we can help the environment by living simpler: we can buy fewer things and keep things we buy longer. We can also use public transportation and only use cars and planes when necessary; we can eat locally-produced food to cut down on transportation costs; and we can recycle more. People with their own houses and gardens can compost their food, grow organic vegetables, and invest in solar panels to provide energy.

[3] However, not everyone agrees that the responsibility for protecting the environment lies with individuals. They point out that most environmental destruction is caused by companies, not individual people. For example, many people are worried that widespread use of fertilizers and pesticides threatens wildlife and pollutes soil and water, and that cutting down forests destroys the habitats of birds and animals. Also, pollution of the sea is often caused by waste from factories or by spills from oil tankers, and scientists warn that overfishing by large commercial fishing fleets could lead to fish disappearing from our oceans. Some people believe these things can only be changed by introducing new laws, not by asking individuals to change their lifestyle.

[4] My own view is that both of these opinions are correct. We can do a lot as individuals to help the environment by behaving in a more responsible way, but that is not enough. We also need governments to take action to reduce pollution and improve the environment, and rich countries should lead the way in doing that.

2 READING

a Leon wrote an essay discussing the topic of protecting the environment. Read the essay and answer the questions.

1 Which of these sentences best summarizes the essay?
   a Leon considers whether individuals or governments can do the most to protect the environment.
   b Leon describes different ways in which we are damaging the environment.
2 What is Leon's conclusion?
   a It's not clear how we can best protect the environment.
   b Both individuals and governments should act to protect the environment.

b Read the essay again and make brief notes on the main points Leon makes.

3 WRITING SKILLS
Arguing for and against an idea

a Match four of the descriptions below to paragraphs 1–4 in the essay.

- Introduction – stating the problem
- Introduction – giving Leon's point of view
- How individuals can help protect the environment
- How large companies damage the environment
- How large companies can help the environment
- Conclusion – restating the problem
- Conclusion – Leon's point of view

b Answer the questions.

1 Why does Leon ask a question in the first paragraph?
2 How does Leon make his arguments seem more objective (i.e., not just his own opinion)?

c Notice how Leon uses expressions like these to report people's opinions.

> It is well known that ...
> Scientists agree that ...

Find more expressions in the essay that:
1 report what other people say or think (x3)
2 report how people feel (x1)
3 report what scientists say (x1)
4 report what Leon thinks himself (x1).

d Write sentences in response to these questions, using expressions from 3c.

Does recycling plastic really make much difference to the environment?
Would eating less meat help protect the environment?
Are pesticides causing bees to die out?

4 WRITING

a Work in pairs. Choose one of the essay topics.

Are extreme weather events a sign of climate change?
Is building nuclear power stations the best way to provide "clean" energy?
Should airfares be increased to discourage people from traveling by plane?

b 💬 Discuss the topic you chose and take notes on possible arguments for and against. Then decide on your conclusion.

c Work on your own. Plan your essay using the structure in 3a.

d 💬 Compare your notes with your partner and explain roughly what you plan to write.

e Write the essay in about 150–200 words, using expressions in 3c.

f Swap essays with another student. Does the essay ... ?

1 have a clear structure
2 set out the arguments in a clear way
3 use suitable expressions for reporting opinions

Do you agree with the conclusion?

UNIT 5
Review and extension

1 GRAMMAR

a Change these sentences using the words in parentheses so that the meaning stays the same.

1 Cities will probably become more dangerous over the next 50 years. (likely)
2 Scientists will probably find a way to delay the aging process soon. (chance)
3 It's likely that the Democratic Party will win the election. (probably)
4 There are bears in this forest, but you probably won't see one. (unlikely)

b Complete the blanks with the verbs in parentheses. Use either future continuous (*will be* + *-ing*) or future perfect (*will have* + past participle).

I'm in my 20s, but I sometimes imagine my life at 70. When I'm 70, I'll ¹_____ (retire), so I won't ²_____ (work) and I'll have plenty of free time. But I will ³_____ (have) a successful career, and I will ⁴_____ (save) a lot of money, so I'll be rich. I will ⁵_____ (get) married in my 30s, and we will ⁶_____ (have) two or three children. By the time we're 70, we'll have a nice house by the ocean, and our children will ⁷_____ (live) nearby.
Of course, my life could turn out differently, but it's always good to have positive dreams!

c 💬 Imagine yourself 30 years from now. What will you be doing? What will you have done by then?

2 VOCABULARY

a What adjective could describe these people? Use words from the box.

well-organized   critical   adventurous
reliable   sympathetic   realistic

1 Dana has started a rock group, but she knows she probably won't ever become famous.
2 Mia always keeps her desk clean, and she knows where to find everything.
3 Tom listens to people's problems and knows how to make them feel better.
4 Pedro gave up work for six months to travel through Central America on a motorcycle.
5 Christine's very hard to please. If you get something wrong, she'll notice it and she'll tell you.
6 If you ask Hamid to do a job, he'll always do it well and on time.

b What is the opposite of these words?

1 reliable   3 responsible   5 well-organized
2 sensitive   4 thoughtful   6 realistic

c 💬 Work in pairs. Which words in 2b (or their opposites) are true of people you know? Tell your partner and give a few examples of things the people do or don't do.

3 WORDPOWER *side*

a Look at these examples and match the word *side* with the meanings in the box.

group or team   point of view   part of a person's character

1 She's friendly, but she also has a rather unpleasant **side**.
2 He usually plays for San Jose, but today he's playing for the other **side**.
3 We need to look at both **sides** of the argument.

b Here are some common expressions with *side*. Use them instead of the underlined parts of the sentences.

on your side   look on the bright side
to one side   from side to side   on the side
side by side   see the funny side

1 They sat on the bench next to each other without talking.
2 We think he was wrong. We're all supporting you.
3 Well, let's see things positively – we're both still alive.
4 I didn't earn much as a taxi driver, but I made a lot of money doing other work.
5 I was very embarrassed at the time, but now I can laugh about what happened.
6 She took me away from the other people and said quietly, "I'll call you tonight."
7 As the sea got rougher, the lamp in my cabin started swinging from left to right.

c Read these extracts from stories. Which sentences in 3b do you think go in the blanks?

1 The first few days of the voyage were calm, but then the weather changed. _____
I lay in my bed watching it, feeling sick.

2 She saw a man approaching. It was Tom. "OK if I sit here?" he asked. She nodded. _____
Then he turned to her and said, "Do you still have the letter?"

d Work in pairs. Choose another sentence from 3b. Imagine it's from a story, and write a sentence before and after it.

e 💬 Read out your sentences. Which were the most interesting?

a Read the texts and check your answers to 1f on p. 24.

Wolf

If you see a wolf before it sees you, walk away silently. If the wolf sees you, back away slowly and avoid eye contact. Wolves see eye contact as a challenge. If the wolf runs toward you, don't run away because wolves are faster than you. Instead, turn to face the wolf. If the wolf attacks you, curl up in a ball, or defend yourself with a stick. A wolf's nose is very sensitive, so if you hit it on the nose it will probably run away. Wolves are also easy to distract with food, so if you have some food, throw it to the wolf, then move slowly away, still facing the wolf.

Shark

Don't lie on the surface of the water in areas where there are sharks because this makes you look like a seal. Instead, try to stay vertical in the water. Sharks normally won't attack unless they smell your blood or they think you're food. So if a shark comes toward you, keep still or swim slowly toward the shark. As long as you don't panic, it will probably swim away. If the shark bites you, hit it in the eye.

Bear

In bear country, always wear a bell or hit trees with a stick to make a noise. This will make any bears that are near go away. If a bear comes toward you, lie on the ground and "play dead." Provided you stay absolutely still, the bear will lose interest. If you are on a hill, run away downhill, going from side to side. Bears find it hard to run fast downhill because they are so heavy and they can't turn quickly.

b Imagine that you had to encounter one of these three animals. Which would you prefer? Why?

c Now go back to p. 24.

a Read about Sharon Tirabassi. Use these questions and keywords to help you focus on the main points.

1 What was Sharon's life like before she won the lottery?
2 How much did she win?
3 What did she do then? (shopping, house, cars)
4 Who did she give money to? (family, friends)
5 What's her life like now? (house, bike, work)
6 Why is she happier now? (lifestyle, kids)

Sharon Tirabassi

Fifteen years ago, Sharon Tirabassi won $10.5 million in the lottery, but you wouldn't know it if you met her now. She lives in a rented house, she works part time as a cleaner, and she doesn't even own a car. So her lifestyle is pretty much the way it used to be before her incredible lottery win.

When Tirabassi, who used to live in a small apartment in Hamilton in Canada, won the lottery, she thought all her problems were over. Suddenly, she was able to live the lifestyle of a millionaire. She would go on extravagant vacations in the Caribbean. She would buy anything she wanted, whether or not she needed it. She also spent a fortune on a huge house and four cars.

But she was also extremely generous to others. She gave about $3 million to her family and bought houses that she rented cheaply to poor families. Not surprisingly, people took advantage of her generosity. Many of the people she loaned money to disappeared without paying her back.

Eventually, the money ran out, and the extravagant lifestyle disappeared with it. She doesn't live in a huge house anymore, but rents a modest house in the area where she grew up, with just a few family photos on the walls.

But Sharon Tirabassi says she doesn't regret what happened. She claims to be happier now than she used to be. Whereas before she would spend her time buying things, other things have now become more important to her. Her main concern is making sure her children grow up with good values. She wants them to learn that they have to work for a living. She has put money into a bank account for them – but they can't access it until they turn 26.

b Now go back to p. 44.

a Prepare to give an opinion on one of the topics below. Plan what you will say about it.

- a recent sports event
- your classroom
- a famous person

b Tell Student B your opinion about the topic you have chosen.

c Listen to Student B's opinion about their topic. Express careful disagreement. Use language in 4c on p. 51.

d Now go back to p. 51.

a Look at the photos of Bogotá, Colombia. Imagine you visited this place. Prepare to present your photos to other students. Decide:

- what the photos show
- what you will say about them
- which expressions in 2a on p. 50 you can use.

Notes: The photos show Plaza de Bolívar in the heart of Bogotá, a bicycle tour of city murals, and your favorite café.

b ≫ Now go back to p. 50.

a You're opening a café in your town. You want it to be different from other cafés. Take notes about:

- furniture
- food and drinks
- music and entertainment
- special things you could offer.

b 💬 Explain your ideas and respond to other students' ideas. Use language from 6a and 6c on p. 63.

c ≫ Now go back to p. 63.

a Read about Ihsan Khan. Use these questions and keywords to help you focus on the main points.

1 What was Khan's life like before his win? (job, money)
2 What was his dream? (diamonds, number)
3 How much did he win?
4 What did he do then? (taxi, car, houses, Pakistan, mayor)
5 Then what happened? (earthquake, medicine, school)
6 Why wasn't he satisfied? (money, greedy)
7 What happened later? (election, votes)

Ihsan Khan

Before he won the lottery, Ihsan Khan used to work as a taxi driver and security guard in the U.S. – first in Chicago and then in Washington. He would usually send most of what he earned back to his family in Pakistan. "It was the worst job in the world," Khan says now. And then, one night, he had a dream in which he saw diamonds and also a number: 2461725. He played those numbers on the lottery for 10 years. Then one day he got lucky. Ihsan Khan won the jackpot, and suddenly he had $55 million. He immediately gave up his job as a taxi driver and bought an expensive car and two luxury houses.

But then he did something surprising. Instead of staying in the U.S. and spending the money on luxuries, he went back to his hometown of Battagram and ran in an election to become mayor. He saw it as a way to pay back some of what he'd gained. Khan believes that it's wrong to save money for yourself and that we have a responsibility to help others who are not as well off as we are. Although he was competing against a candidate whose family had been in local politics for 35 years, Khan was elected mayor. Then, just after he was elected, the region was hit by a huge earthquake which killed 3,000 people in Battagram. Mayor Khan took the opportunity to use his lottery money to help people directly. He spent $300,000 on medicine and on repairs to homes, and he also gave money to build a new school.

But Khan wasn't fully satisfied and felt that just giving people money wasn't enough. He used to think he could use his money to fix everything, but he no longer believes that. He discovered that people are often greedy, and they never seem satisfied with what they are given.

In 2008, he resigned as mayor and ran for election to the Pakistan parliament, but this time he wasn't a winner. The winning candidate received over 22,000 votes. Ihsan Khan only received 5,000. It seems his luck had run out.

b ≫ Now go back to p. 44.

a 💬 You need to buy a new jacket. You'd like Student B to come with you after class, because you need someone's advice on the best jacket to buy. You're not sure if Student B likes to go shopping. Perhaps suggest doing something nice as well, for example going out for coffee together. Make careful suggestions and try to agree on what you can do after class.

b ≫ Now go back to p. 39.

3C STUDENT B

a 💬📢 You'd like to go somewhere fun with Student A after class. You don't really like shopping unless it means going to a store that sells video games. It might be fun to go to a new juice bar that opened last week. You could also go to the movies. Make careful suggestions and try to agree on what you can do after class.

b ⋙ Now go back to p. 39.

4C STUDENT B

a Prepare to give an opinion on one of the topics below. Plan what you will say about it.

- a movie or book
- a café or restaurant
- the town/city you're in now

b 💬📢 Listen to Student A's opinion about their topic. Express careful disagreement. Use language in 4c on p. 51.

c 💬📢 Tell Student A your opinion about the topic you have chosen.

d ⋙ Now go back to p. 51.

5B

a Read the text and check your answers to the quiz in 1b on p. 59.

Antarctica is the fifth largest continent in the world and is completely surrounded by the Southern Ocean. It is approximately the size of the U.S. and Mexico. About 98% of Antarctica is covered by ice that averages 1.6 km in thickness. It is the coldest, driest, and windiest continent in the world. Temperatures reach minimums of between –80 °C and –90 °C in the winter. The landscape is considered a kind of desert because there is very little rainfall. There are mountains, glaciers, and rivers, but no trees or bushes. There is a variety of animal life on the continent, but the two most well known are penguins and seals. The continent is positioned around the southernmost point of the planet, the South Pole. The first person to reach the South Pole was the Norwegian Roald Amundsen.

b ⋙ Now go back to p. 59.

4C STUDENT B

a Look at the photos of Moscow, Russia. Imagine you visited this place. Prepare to present your photos to other students. Decide:

- what the photos show
- what you will say about them
- which expressions in 2a on p. 50 you can use.

Notes: The photos show Moscow State University, built in 1953.

b ⋙ Now go back to p. 50.

5A

a Are you an optimist or a pessimist? Read the descriptions below to find out.

Your answers are mostly on the *Optimist* side of the scale.
You expect things to turn out well for you, and when you encounter problems, you believe you can overcome them. When things go well, you usually see it as the result of your own ability or hard work. When things go badly, you see it as just bad luck and expect it to be better next time.

Your answers are mostly on the *Pessimist* side of the scale.
You don't always expect things to turn out well for you, and when you encounter problems, you believe you are generally unlucky. When things go well, you usually see it as the result of chance or what other people have done. When things go badly, you see it as a result of your own weaknesses.

b ⋙ Now go back to p. 56.

1A Review of tenses

▶ 01.01

Simple present

We use the simple present:

- for habits, repeated actions, facts, and things which are generally true.
  *I usually **do** my homework in the evening.*
  *She **writes** crime stories.*
- with stative verbs for short-term states, verbs of preference, and verbs of the senses.
  *I **want** to go home.*

Present perfect

We use the present perfect:

- for experiences in our life without saying when they happened.
  *I**'ve seen** this movie three times.*
- to focus on present states which started in the past and have continued up to the present.
  *I**'ve lived** here since I was a child.*
- with *yet* in a question to ask if something is complete.
  ***Have** you **sent** it yet?*
- with *already* in affirmative statements to show that something is complete, often before we expected.
  *I**'ve already mailed** your package.*

Present continuous

We use the present continuous:

- for actions in progress now (at the moment of speaking) or around now.
  *Sorry, I can't talk now – I**'m doing** my homework.*
  *She**'s writing** a book about her life.*

- for temporary situations.
  *I**'m studying** English in Toronto this semester, but normally I work in São Paulo.*

Simple past

We use the simple past:

- to talk about completed past actions and states. We often specify the time in the past with the simple past:
  *I **lost** my phone last week, but then I **found** it in my car.*

Past perfect

We use the past perfect:

- for actions and events that happened before a particular moment in time.
- for reasons (after *because*).
  *I decided to walk home because I **had forgotten** my bus pass.*

Past continuous

We use the past continuous:

- to describe actions that were in progress at a particular moment in the past.
- for actions or events in progress at the time of a shorter, simple past action.
  *He called while I **was doing** my homework.*

1B Questions

▶ 01.12 **Affirmative and negative questions**

Most questions have an auxiliary verb (e.g., *be, do, have,* or modal verbs) before the subject. The auxiliary verb can be affirmative or negative:

*How **do** you spell that?*   *Why **isn't** my computer working?*

Prepositions usually come at the end of questions.
*Where are you **from**? NOT ~~From where are you?~~*

In very formal questions they can go at the beginning.

> 🔎 **Tip** We can make short questions from *who / what / where* + preposition:
> **A** *I'm going to a party tonight.*   **B** *Who with?*
> **A** *Can I borrow your phone?*   **B** *What for? (Why?)*

We use negative questions to express surprise:
***Haven't** they **finished** yet?* (I'm surprised)

When we ask about the subject of a sentence, the word order doesn't change and we don't use an auxiliary verb.
***Somebody** wrote this book.* → ***Who** wrote this book?*
NOT ~~Who did write this book?~~

▶ 01.13 **Indirect questions**

We use indirect questions to sound polite. Start indirect questions with *Can you tell me... / Do you know...* We don't use an auxiliary verb and the word order doesn't change: Use *if* in indirect *Yes / No* questions.

*Why **did she become** famous?* → ***Do you know why** she became famous?*

***Do you know** if the museum is open?* → ***Can you tell me if** the museum is open?*

We can also use indirect questions in sentences starting with: *I'm not sure ... I know / don't know ... I wonder ... I can't remember ...* etc.

Is this answer correct? → *I**'m not sure** if this answer is correct.*
Where have they been? → *I **wonder** where they've been.*

> 🔎 **Tip** We use **which** + **noun** when there is a limited number of options and **what** + **noun** when there are many possibilities:
> *We can have our meeting at 10:00, 12:15, or 2:30. **Which time** would you prefer?*
> *I'm free all day. **What time** do you want to meet?*

1A Review of tenses

a Correct the mistakes in the sentences. Think about spelling, tense, and form.

1 I'm ~~studing~~ hard at the moment because ~~I try~~ to pass my final exams.   *studying, I'm trying*
2 Internet shopping becomes more and more popular these days.   _____
3 We looking for new members for our group. Do you want to join?   _____
4 This food is tasting a bit strange. I think I prefer food from my own country.   _____
5 We think of buying a new car, but they're costing a lot of money.   _____
6 I write to apply for the job of sales assistant. I send my C.V. with this letter.   _____

b Match the sentence halves.

1 ☐ When I arrived, …   a … I was watching television.
2 ☐ While my brother was cooking, …   b … twice in my life.
3 ☐ I was waiting for the plumber …   c … Sally had already left.
4 ☐ I have been to Machu Picchu …   d … when he called me to cancel.
5 ☐ Robert stayed in my apartment …   e … in 2018 to work abroad for a year.
6 ☐ I moved to Singapore …   f … both this summer and last summer, too.

c ⟫ Now go back to p. 9.

1B Questions

a Choose the best word or phrase to complete each question.

1 Where *we are / are we* going to eat?
2 What *you thought / did you think* of the movie? Did you enjoy it?
3 We have cheese sandwiches and egg sandwiches. *What / Which* one do you prefer?
4 Why *you didn't / didn't you* call me?
5 I hear you're a musician. *What / Which* kind of music do you play?
6 **A** I got this watch for my birthday. **B** *Who from? / What from?*
7 What *happened / was happened* to the window?

b Write questions about the underlined words and phrases.

1 _____*Who discovered pulsars?*_____   Jocelyn Bell-Burnell discovered pulsars.
2 _____   She's interested in classical music.
3 _____   Over 2,000 people watched the game.
4 _____   They haven't started yet because they're waiting for you.
5 _____   My left foot hurts.
6 _____   She heard the news from Ralph.

c Rewrite the sentences and questions using the prompts.

1 What do you want?
   I don't know …   _____*what you want.*_____
2 Why didn't they come back?
   I wonder …   _____
3 Where are they going?
   Where do you think …   _____
4 Have you ever met him?
   Can you tell me …   _____
5 Who wrote this story?
   Do you know …   _____
6 Does this pen work?
   I wonder …   _____
7 What's your sister's name?
   Can you tell me …   _____
8 When will it be ready?
   When do you think …   _____

d ⟫ Now go back to p. 13.

2A Narrative tenses

We use narrative tenses to tell stories about what happened in the past. The most important narrative tenses are simple past, past continuous, past perfect, and past perfect continuous.

▶ 02.06

We use the simple past for completed past actions and states which happened at a specific time in the past:
*We **spotted** them on the mountain, so we **rescued** them and **took** them to the hospital.*

We use the past continuous for actions (not states) that were in progress at the time of the main events in the story:
*When we spotted them, they **were standing** next to some stones. They **were waving** their arms, but we couldn't hear what they **were shouting**.*

We use the past perfect / past perfect continuous for events and activities that happened before the main events in the story and to give explanations or reasons. It often occurs after *because*.
*We spotted them because they **had built** the word "HELP" out of stones.*
*We finally spotted them after we **had been searching** for over a week.*

Past perfect or past perfect continuous?

We use the past perfect:
- To focus on the results of an earlier completed action:
  *We **spotted** them (result) because they**'d built** a big sign (earlier action).*
- To talk about "time up to then" with a <u>stative</u> verb (e.g., *know, have, be*):
  *When we found them, they**'d been** on the mountain for a week.*

We use the past perfect continuous:
- before a result in the past to show the effect of an earlier activity:
  *They **were tired** (result) because they**'d been building** a big sign (earlier activity).*
- To emphasize the duration of time with an <u>action</u> verb (e.g., *wait, search, drive*):
  *We found them after we**'d been searching** for a week.*

After we**'d been searching** for them for over a week, we finally **spotted** them on the mountain. They **were** standing next to the word 'HELP' which **they'd built** out of stones.

we searched   we spotted them

Past   they built the word   they stood   Future

2B Future time clauses and conditionals

We use future time clauses to talk about future possibilities, future plans, or to give advice. We can normally use *will, be going to,* or the imperative in the main clause.

We normally use a present tense in the subordinate clause with words like *if, when, as soon as, unless, as long as, provided, in case,* etc. We can also use the same time clauses to talk about facts and things which are generally true. In these sentences we often use a present tense verb in the main clause.

▶ 02.07

***When** we **go** hiking next weekend, we'll try a new trail.*
***If** you **see** a bear, don't run.*
*It won't attack you **as long as** you**'re standing** still.*
***Unless** you know the way, **bring** a map.*
*Always bring a snack **in case** you **get** hungry.*
***As soon as** it **gets** too cold, we'll go home.*

> ☿ **Tip**
>
> When *if* means *whether*, we normally need *will* or *going to* to refer to the future:
> *I don't know **if / whether** I**'ll** see any wild animals when I'm on vacation. NOT: ... ~~if I see~~ ...*

▶ 02.08 *as soon as*

As soon as shows that something will happen immediately after another thing:
***As soon as** I get home, I'll email you.*

> ☿ **Tip**
>
> We can use simple present or present perfect after words like *as soon as* or *when* to talk about completed processes in the future. There is little difference in meaning:
> *We'll leave **when / as soon as I finish** my work. (Or: ... **I've finished** ...)*

▶ 02.09 *if, unless, as long as, provided,* and *in case*

Unless means *if not*. The verb after *unless* is usually affirmative:
*You won't see any animals **unless** you **stay** quiet.* (You won't see any animals if you don't stay quiet).

As long as and *provided* are similar to *only if*:
*We'll be safe **provided / as long as** we stay here.* (But only if we stay here).
*You can go out tonight **as long as** you're back by 10.* (But only if you're back by 10).

We use *in case* to talk about preparations for possible future situations:
*Take your keys **in case** we're out when you get home.*

Don't worry! She **won't** attack you **unless** she **thinks** you're scared.

2A Narrative tenses

a Complete the sentences with the simple past or past continuous form of the verbs in parentheses.

1 While he __was walking__ (walk) in the forest, he __tripped__ (trip) and __cut__ (cut) his knee.

2 I _____ (not / notice) what the thief _____ (wear) because I _____ (hide) under the desk the whole time.

3 When I _____ (get) home, everyone _____ (watch) TV. Nobody _____ (even / say) "Hello."

4 **A** Where _____ (you / be) when you _____ (hear) the news?
B I _____ (be) on the bus – I _____ (travel) to work.

5 Fortunately, I _____ (not / hurt) myself when I _____ (fall) because I _____ (wear) a helmet.

6 **A** What page number _____ (the teacher / just / say)?
B Sorry, I _____ (not / hear) anything. I _____ (not / listen).

b Choose the best verb forms.

1 She was out of breath because *she'd run / she'd been running*.

2 It was sad to sell my old car – *I'd had / I'd been having* it since I was a student.

3 The party was great. *They'd planned / They'd been planning* it for months.

4 We were really pleased because *we'd finished / we'd been finishing* our project.

5 The race was canceled because it *had rained / had been raining* for days and the streets were flooded.

6 How long *had they known / had they been knowing* each other when they decided to get married?

7 They weren't very happy because *they'd waited / they'd been waiting* for six hours.

8 I didn't watch the movie because *I'd already seen / I'd already been seeing* it four times.

c Choose the best verb forms.

It [1]*happened / had happened* on the last day of our vacation. We [2]*were getting / got* up and [3]*saw / were seeing* that, at last, the sun [4]*was shining / had shone*. We [5]*were leaving / left* the hotel and [6]*were starting / started* walking along the narrow cliff path. Then, after [7]*we'd been walking / we walked* for about two hours, the path [8]*was suddenly becoming / suddenly became* much narrower – it was no more than 10 cm wide. There [9]*had been being / had been* a storm the previous night, and the sea [10]*had washed / was washing* part of the path away.

The cliff wasn't very high, so [11]*we'd decided / we decided* to keep going, along the narrow path. I [12]*went / was going* first, and [13]*had made / made* it safely to the other side. But then I [14]*was hearing / heard* a shout and a splash. Mike [15]*had fallen / fell* into the sea below. There were sharp rocks all around him, but luckily [16]*he'd landed / he'd been landing* safely in the water, and [17]*wasn't hurting / hadn't hurt* himself. So I [18]*climbed / was climbing* down the cliff to help him to safety.

Later, back at the hotel, he [19]*had been explaining / explained* what had gone wrong: [20]*he'd been trying / he tried* to take a selfie at the time of his fall.

d ≫ Now go back to p. 22.

2B Future time clauses and conditionals

a Check (✓) the correct sentences. Correct the mistakes.

1 ☐ I'll send you a postcard when ~~we'll be~~ on vacation. *incorrect   we're*
2 ✓ We'll come out as soon as we finish dinner.
3 ☐ My parents don't mind if I go out as long as I'll tell them where I'm going.
4 ☐ You won't pass the exam unless you don't study harder.
5 ☐ If it's still raining when you'll finish work, I'll pick you up.
6 ☐ I'm going to leave my laptop at home in case it'll get damaged.
7 ☐ I lend you my car provided you won't drive too fast.

b Connect the sentences using the words in parentheses.

1 Maybe I'll see Joseph. I'll tell him to call you. (if)
2 She'll finish college. She wants to be a teacher. (when)
3 They'll be late if they don't hurry up. (unless)
4 I'll check your work. Then I'll send it back to you immediately. (as soon as)
5 You can take photographs but you can't use a flash. (provided)
6 You should take some money because you might need to take a taxi. (in case)
7 He won't bite you, but you must be careful. (as long as)
8 You'll only understand if you listen very carefully. (unless)

I'll __tell Joseph to call you if I see him.__
She _____
They'll _____
I'll _____
You _____
You _____
As _____
You _____

c ≫ Now go back to p. 24.

3A Multi-word verbs

▶ 03.03 Multi-word verbs consist of a verb and one or two particles:
*We **came up with** some good ideas and decided to **try** them **out**.*

Sometimes the meaning of the multi-word verb is clear from the meaning of the verb and the particle (e.g., *sit down*), but often you have to learn the meaning of each multi-word verb.

Transitive and intransitive multi-word verbs

- Transitive multi-word verbs need an object. The object can come before the particle (e.g., *throw **sth** away*) or after the particle (e.g., *look after **sb***), depending on the type of multi-word verb.
- Intransitive multi-word verbs don't have an object, e.g., *go away* NOT ~~go somebody away~~.

Type 1 has no direct object (intransitive): verb + particle	wake up; go away; fall down; stay up; break up; sit down; take off; calm down
Type 2 has an object (transitive): verb + noun/pronoun + particle OR verb + particle + noun/pronoun	wake sb up; take sth off, calm sb down; try sth out; figure sth out; make sth up; throw sth away; pick sth up; let sb down
Type 3 has an object (transitive): verb + particle + noun/pronoun	look into sth; focus on sth; believe in sth; live for sth; be into sth; look after sb
Type 4 has two particles and always has an object: verb + particle 1 + particle 2 + noun/pronoun	come up with sth; look down on sb; look up to sb; run out of sth; fall down on sth; fall out with sb; go on about sth; get away with sth

🗨 **Tip** Many multi-word verbs are both transitive and intransitive (e.g., *wake up; fall down; take off; calm down*):
*When you **wake up** (intransitive), try not to **wake the dog up** (transitive), too!*
*After the plane **took off** (intransitive), I **took my shoes off** (transitive).* Use a dictionary to find out if a multi-word verb is transitive or intransitive.

Type 2 multi-word verbs
When the object is a long noun phrase, it normally comes after the particle:
*Please **throw away** those old shoes that are nearly falling apart!*
When the object is a pronoun (e.g., *it, me, sb*), it almost always comes before the particle:
*Those shoes are really old. Please **throw** them **away**!* NOT: ~~Please **throw away them**!~~
When the object is a short noun phrase (e.g., up to three words), it can come before or after the particle:
*Please **throw** those old shoes **away** / Please **throw away** those old shoes.*

3B Present perfect and present perfect continuous

▶ 03.08 We use the **present perfect**:
- to talk about experiences without saying when they happened
  *He**'s tried** to run a marathon four times in his life.*
- for experiences during any present period of time
  *What **have** you **learned** so far **this year**?*
- with superlatives
  *She**'s the nicest person** I**'ve** ever **met**.*
- with *already* and *yet*
  *I**'ve already put** the food in the oven, but I **haven't set** the table **yet**.*
- to talk about *how long* with stative verbs (with *for / since*)
  *I**'ve known** them **for** years, but I **haven't seen** them **since** January.*
- with *how many, how much,* and *how often* to talk about experiences
  How many essays have you written?

We use the **present perfect continuous:**
- when a recently completed action has a result now
  *She's tired because she**'s been training** hard.*
- to describe repeated activities which started recently
  *I**'ve been going** to the gym a lot recently.*
- to talk about unfinished activities using *how long* and *for / since*
  *We**'ve been walking since** the sun came up.*

3A Multi-word verbs

a Choose the correct sentences. Sometimes more than one sentence is correct.

1 a I don't **believe in** these new language learning techniques.
  b I don't **believe** these new language learning techniques **in**.
  c I don't **believe in** them.
  d I don't **believe** them **in**.

2 a Do you want **to** try the new guitar I got for my birthday **out**?
  b Do you want to **try out** the new guitar I got for my birthday?
  c Do you want to **try out** it?
  d Do you want to **try it out**?

3 a We **fell out with** our neighbors.
  b We **fell with** our neighbors **out**.
  c We **fell** them **out with**.
  d We **fell out with** them.

4 a Did you **make up** that story?
  b Did you **make** that story **up**?
  c Did you **make up** it?
  d Did you **make it up**?

b Rewrite these sentences replacing the verbs in **bold** with multi-word verbs.
Use a verb from A and one or two particles from B.

A

| ~~come~~ be go take look let figure run |

B

| ~~up~~ into out off about of ~~with~~ into out down on |

1 How did you **invent** a name for your shop? *How did you come up with a name for your shop?*
2 Have you **investigated** the cause of the accident?
3 I've **liked** jazz since I was in college.
4 I hope we don't **use all of** this food.
5 I hate to **disappoint** you.
6 I can't **understand** it.
7 I know I was wrong. Stop **repeating** it!
8 Do you think this product will **be successful**?

c ≫ Now go back to p. 34.

3B Present perfect and present perfect continuous

a What are the most likely combinations? Match the sentence halves.

1 ☐ I'm really proud of myself because …
2 ☐ I'm exhausted lately because …
  a … I've been building a wall in my garden.
  b … I'm learning how to build a wall in my garden.

3 ☐ They've been on vacation …
4 ☐ They've been going on vacation …
  a … three times this year.
  b … to the same place for 20 years.

5 ☐ I've written …
6 ☐ I've been writing …
  a … six emails already.
  b … emails all morning.

7 ☐ She's been playing …
8 ☐ She's played …
  a … tennis twice this week.
  b … a lot of tennis recently.

b Check (✓) the correct sentences. Correct the mistakes.

1 ✓ How long have you worked here?
2 ☐ Please don't come in – we ~~haven't been finishing~~ yet. *incorrect   haven't finished*
3 ☐ Have you ever been sailing?
4 ☐ We've been giving three presentations this week.
5 ☐ This room has been empty since our son left home.
6 ☐ I've been watching a lot of movies lately … maybe too many.
7 ☐ I haven't been hearing that old song since I was a child.
8 ☐ Those people have been calling me five times today.

c Complete the sentences with the correct form of the verbs in parentheses. Use the present perfect or the present perfect continuous.

1 I *'ve already spent* (already / spend) over $500 on soccer lessons for you, and now you're saying you don't like soccer!
2 Can you hurry up? We _____ (wait) for so long!
3 How long _____ (you / study) to become a doctor?
4 She _____ (not / say) a word all day – I think she's angry with me.
5 _____ (you / clean) the car yet, or is it still dirty?
6 **A** Your eyes are red. _____? (you / cry) **B** No, I _____ (chop) onions!

d ≫ Now go back to p. 37.

4A *used to* and *would*

▶ 04.01 *used to* and *would*

We often use *used to* to describe past situations. In general, these situations continued for a long time and are not true now. They can be states (e.g., *like, live, have*) or habits (= repeated actions):
*When I was a child, I **didn't use to** like vegetables, but now I love them.*
*When we were students, we **used to** go dancing every week.*

We can also use *would* to describe past habits. Don't use *would* for past states:
*When we were students, we**'d go** dancing every week.*

We often use a mixture of *used to, would,* and the simple past when talking about our past:
*When I was young, we never **used to** go on vacation. Instead, we**'d spend** the whole summer playing in the fields near our house. We **loved** it.*

> **Tip** Don't use *used to* or *would* for things that happened only once, or when we say how many times something happened in the past:
> *I read that book **once** / **a few times** when I was a teenager.* NOT *I used to read …*

▶ 04.02 *no longer* and *anymore*

We use *no longer* before a positive verb or after *be*:
*We **no longer** go to the old forest. It's **no longer** there.*
We use *anymore* at the end of a sentence with a negative verb:
*We **don't** go to the old forest **anymore**. It's **not** there **anymore**.*

▶ 04.03 *Comparing the past and the present*

We can make comparisons using *used to*:
*She is happier now than she **used to be**.* (= She wasn't very happy before.)
*He works much harder than he **used to**.* (= He works harder now than before.)
*We don't spend as much as we **used to**.* (= Now we spend less than before.)

> **Tip** After *used to*, repeat the verb *be*, but **don't** repeat main verbs:
> *I earn more than I **used to**. (NOT … than **I used to earn**.)*

Before I made my fortune, I**'d** bike to work every day. I really miss that.

4B Obligation and permission

▶ 04.10

	Making a rule	Describing someone else's rule	
		Present	**Past**
Strong affirmative obligation	*You **must** wear a helmet. I won't let you ride without one.*	*We **have to** / **need to** wear a helmet. It's the law.*	*We **had to** / **needed to** wear a helmet to go on the motorcycle.*
Strong negative obligation	*You **must not** / **mustn't** remove your helmet. It's far too dangerous.*	*We**'re not allowed to** / **can't** remove our helmets. The instructor will get very angry with us.*	*We **weren't allowed to** remove our helmets.*
Affirmative obligation	*I think you **should** / **ought to** give the money back.*	*I**'m supposed to** give the money back, but I don't want to.*	*I **was supposed to** give the money back, but I forgot.*
No obligation	*You **don't have to** / **don't need to** buy a ticket.*		*You **didn't have to** / **didn't need to** buy a ticket.*
Permission	*Yes, it's OK, you **can** go home.*	*I **can** / **I'm allowed to** go home now.*	*I **could** / **was allowed to** go home before 5 p.m.*
No permission	*No, I'm sorry. You **cannot** / **can't** go home yet.*	*I **can't** / **I'm not allowed to** go home yet.*	*I **couldn't** / **wasn't allowed to** go home early.*

- *must* and *mustn't* are very strong. In most situations, it's more natural to use *have to, need to, needn't, can't, be not allowed to,* etc. Questions with *must* are very rare.
- *should* is much more common than *ought to*. Questions and negatives with *ought to* are very rare.
- *Need to* is like *have to*, whereas *need* (usually found in the negative) is a modal.

▶ 04.11 *make* and *let*; *be forced to* and *be allowed to*

make and *let* are special because they are followed by an object + infinitive without *to*:
*They **made** me **pay** extra.* NOT *They **made me to pay** extra.*
*They **let** me **come** in for free.* NOT *They **let me to come** in for free.*
We often use the verbs *force* and *allow* in passive constructions. Both are followed by *to* + infinitive:
*I **was forced to** pay extra.* (Less common: *I was made to pay extra.*)
*I **was allowed to** come in for free.* NOT *I was **let come in** for free.*

4A *used to* and *would*

a Check (✓) the possible forms in the sentences. More than one answer is possible.

1 She _____ good at math when she was little.
   a ✓ used to be   b ☐ would be
2 Laura was my best friend – we _____ for hours every day.
   a ☐ used to talk   b ☐ would talk
3 I _____ five swimming competitions when I was in school.
   a ☐ won   b ☐ would win
4 Our teacher, Mr. Williams, was very strict. He _____ allow us to speak at all during class.
   a ☐ didn't use to   b ☐ wouldn't
5 I'll never forget the time I _____ my leg. I couldn't walk for weeks!
   a ☐ used to break   b ☐ broke
6 We _____ a dog, but he died about five years ago.
   a ☐ used to have   b ☐ would have

b Choose the correct forms.

1 I *used to / would* be really good at football when I was young, but now I'm terrible at it.
2 I *didn't use to / didn't used to* like jazz, but now it's my favorite kind of music.
3 They're much fitter than they *used to / used to be*.
4 I don't go out as much as I *used to / used to go*.
5 I *went / used to go* to New York once when I was a child.
6 She's much better at English now than she *would / used to* be.

c ≫ Now go back to p. 45.

4B Obligation and permission

a Rewrite the sentences using the words in parentheses.

1 You can wear whatever you want. (need to)
2 I think you should write to them. (ought)
3 They made me give them my phone. (forced)
4 They won't let you park there. (allowed)
5 You don't have to stay here. (can)
6 They advised us to bring strong shoes. (supposed)
7 I wasn't allowed to use a dictionary. (let)
8 It was raining so we were forced to stop. (made)

_____ You don't need to wear _____ a uniform.
I think _____.
They _____.
You aren't _____.
_____ if you like.
We _____.
They _____.
The rain _____.

b Look at the rules for a computer training class. Andy explains the rules to his friend Dan. Complete the conversation with one word or a contraction (e.g., *can't*) in each space.

- All users must change their passwords after first logging in.
- You are not allowed to access the computer system without a new password.
- You can choose your own password.
- Your new password must be at least 20 characters long.
- Your password should be easy to remember, but it shouldn't be easy to guess.
- You must not tell anyone else your password.

Dan: So how was the class?
Andy: It was OK, but the security was really strict. We ¹___ had / needed ___ to change our password right away.
Dan: Why?
Andy: They said we ²_____ access the system without a new one. We were ³_____ to choose our own passwords, but it ⁴_____ to contain at least 20 characters.
Dan: Wow … that's long!
Andy: Yes, but it was ⁵_____ to be something that's easy to remember.
Dan: OK, so the name of your soccer team then?
Andy: No, it was ⁶_____ to be something that's not easy to guess.
Dan: So what was it?
Andy: I ⁷_____ tell you! We're not ⁸_____ to tell anyone else!

c ≫ Now go back to p. 49.

5A Future probability

We use a wide range of modals verbs, adverbs, adjectives, etc., to describe what we think is the probability of future events:

Degree of probability	Modal verbs	Other expressions	Adjectives
 100% high	*We **will** go.* *We **will certainly** go.*	***I'm sure** we'll go.*	*It's **certain** that we'll go.*
	*We **will probably** go.* *We **will likely** go.*		*It's (very) **likely** that we'll go.*
50% medium	*We **could** go.* *We **may** go.* *We **might** go.*	***There's a (good) chance** that we'll go.*	*It's **possible** that we'll go.*
	*We **probably won't** go.*	*I **don't think** we'll go.* *I **doubt if** we'll go.*	*It's (very) **unlikely** that we'll go.*
0% low	*We **won't** go.* *We **certainly won't** go.*	***There's no chance** that we'll go.* *I **can't imagine** that we'll go.*	

05.06 Affirmative and negative forms

We can make negative statements of probability with *might not* or *may not*. Don't use *couldn't* in this way – it refers to the past ability, not future probability:

We **could** *go out on Friday.* (= it's possible that we'll go out next Friday.)
We **couldn't** *go out on Friday.* (= we weren't able to go out last Friday.)

Adverbs like *certainly* and *probably* increase or decrease the level of certainty and come after *will*, but they come before *won't*:
*It'**ll probably** be a nice day today, but it **probably won't** be nice tomorrow.*

05.07 Adjective + *to* + infinitive

With the adjectives *sure / likely / unlikely / certain / bound* we can use the pattern: *be* + adjective + *to* + infinitive:

*They'**re sure to be** late.* (= I'm sure that they'll be late.)
*He'**s certain / likely / unlikely to see** you.*
*There'**s bound to be** someone who knows the answer.*
(= I'm sure someone knows the answer.)

5B Future perfect and future continuous

05.09 Future perfect

Affirmative	Negative	Question	Short answer
We'll have left.	She won't have left.	Will they have left?	Yes, they will / No, they won't.

We use the future perfect to describe what we expect to happen before a specific time in the future:
*I don't know exactly when somebody will buy my car. I hope **I'll have sold** it by the end of the month.*

Tip We often use future perfect with *by*.
*We'll have finished **by Friday / by the time** they get here.*

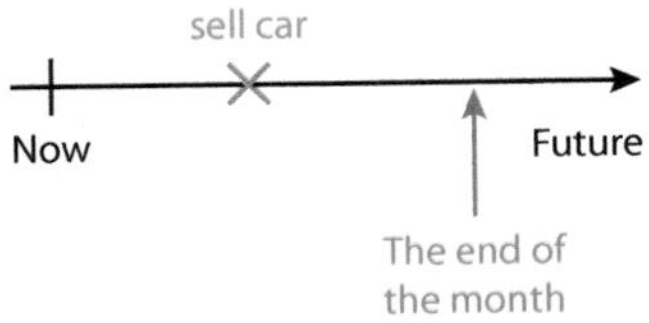
sell car
Now
Future
The end of the month

I don't know exactly when somebody will buy my car.
I hope **I'll have sold** it by the end of the month.

05.10 Future continuous

Affirmative	Negative	Question	Short answer
He'll be driving.	We won't be driving.	Will you be driving?	Yes, I will / No, I won't.

We use the future continuous for activities that will be in progress around a particular time in the future:
*Don't call me at 5 p.m. **I'll** still **be driving** home from work at that time.*

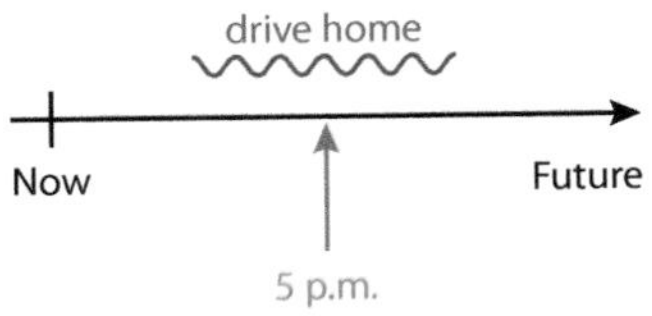
drive home
Now
Future
5 p.m.

We can also use future continuous for things that are already planned:
*It'll be tough in my new job – **I'll be getting** up at 4 a.m. every day.*

5A Future probability

a Complete the sentences with the words from the box. Use each word once.

can't chance if likely might no
probably don't think sure

1 I'll _probably_ get up at about 8 a.m. tomorrow.
2 I don't _____ I'll ever see them again.
3 It's very _____ that you'll get a better job soon.
4 I _____ imagine that they'll move to another country.
5 There's _____ chance that we'll win, but we can try.
6 That _____ be the best idea.
7 I'm _____ you'll have a wonderful time.
8 I _____ think too many people will be interested.
9 There's a good _____ that I'll be back before 10.
10 I doubt _____ they'll be able to fix my printer.

b Rewrite the sentences using the words in parentheses. Keep the meaning the same as the original.

1 It's certain that he'll pay you. (to)
  He's _____ _certain to pay you._
2 It's very unlikely that we'll leave. (probably)
  We_____.
3 He'll certainly win a medal. (bound)
  He's _____.
4 These new phones are probably not going to sell well. (unlikely)
  It's _____.
5 It's possible that she won't notice. (might)
  She _____.
6 I'm sure there'll be another chance. (to be)
  There's _____.

c ⟫ Now go back to p. 58.

5B Future perfect and future continuous

a Check (✓) the correct sentences. Fix the mistakes.

1 ☐ I'd prefer to visit you in August because ~~I'll be finishing~~ my exams then.   _incorrect_   _I'll have finished_
2 ☐ I don't want to be late – they'll have eaten all the food before we get there!   _____
3 ☐ I can't take you to the airport at 10 because I'll have attended a very important meeting at that time.   _____
4 ☐ The presentation is scheduled for the 15th, so I'm sure I'll be writing it then.   _____
5 ☐ Thursday is the best day to call me at home because I'll have worked from home then.   _____
6 ☐ I can pass the message on to Arthur – I'll be seeing him tomorrow at college.   _____
7 ☐ **A** How will I recognize you at the airport?
    B I'll have carried a sign with your name on it.   _____
8 ☐ **A** I can't access the Internet right now.
    B Try again in 10 minutes – hopefully it'll be working again then.   _____

b Look at Christina's calendar for tomorrow. Complete her conversation with Zofia with the future continuous or future perfect form of the verb in parentheses.

ZOFIA So, what time can I come and visit you tomorrow? How about 8:30?
CHRISTINA No, sorry, [1]___I'll still be taking___ (I / still / take) the kids to school at that time.
ZOFIA OK, so maybe when you're back home. [2]_____ (you / get) back by 9:30?
CHRISTINA Yes, probably. But [3]_____ (I / still / deal) with my emails then. I have some urgent emails that I need to reply to. But you could come at about 11. I'm sure [4]_____ (I / finish) by then. Does that work for you?
ZOFIA Er … not really. Could we make it a bit later? How about 2:00?
CHRISTINA Yes, that's fine, but it'll only give us an hour. [5]_____ (I / leave) at 3:00 to pick the kids up from school.
ZOFIA OK, yes, an hour should be perfect. Oh, one thing. Can you lend me that book you were telling me about?
CHRISTINA Well, Hannah has it at the moment. She wants to read it tonight. But [6]_____ (I / see) her tomorrow, so I can ask her to bring it. [7]_____ (she / finish) it by then.

Monday
8:00 – 9:00
Take children to school

9:00 – 10:45(?)
Deal with emails

12:30 – 2:00
Meet Hannah

3:00 – 4:00
Pick up children from school

c ⟫ Now go back to p. 61.

1A Character adjectives

a Read the descriptions of people's characters. Which is personal and which is more formal?

Fred currently works as a researcher here at Bio-Tech. He's been a very **loyal** member of our staff and has worked here for over ten years now. He's **passionate** about alternative energies, and this can be seen in the energy and enthusiasm he puts into his work. He's also **self-confident**, so he is never afraid to work independently or to work on difficult tasks. Finally, he's always **optimistic**, even when he comes across problems in his work.

We have this new colleague at work, Sheila. She's only been here for two weeks and already I don't like her very much. She's one of those **ambitious** people who has a lot of plans, but she's so **arrogant** about it all. She thinks she's better than everyone else. But if you try and suggest a different idea, she gets really upset. So she's a strange mix of being very sure of herself, but incredibly **sensitive** at the same time. She told me that she wants to be our team leader. If she thinks that's going to happen overnight, she's really **naive**!

b Match the **bold** character adjectives in **a** with the definitions.
1 when you don't have much experience of the world and believe things too easily
2 when you easily get upset by what people say about you
3 when you believe or behave as if you know more or are more important than other people
4 when you feel sure about yourself and your abilities
5 when you like something and have strong feelings about it
6 when you have a strong wish to be successful, powerful, or rich
7 when you always support something or someone, even when other people don't
8 when you always think good things will happen

c ▶01.06 Complete the sentences with the adjectives from the texts in **a**. Listen and check.
1 He's very _____. If I give him any negative feedback, he gets angry and shouts at me.
2 I'm sure he won't be nervous when he gives the speech. He always seems very _____.
3 I feel very _____ that this project will be successful – everything is going according to plan.
4 They both think they're fantastic and everyone else is stupid. I've never met a couple who is so _____.
5 She's helped and supported me since we were in school together. She's a very_____ friend – I know I can always rely on her.
6 Paola is really _____ about being a doctor. She loves the job and looks forward to going to work every day.
7 She works really hard because she's _____ and wants to do well in her career.
8 Martin is a little _____ – he honestly thought his boss would listen to his suggestions, but of course in the end he didn't. He really is very young.

d 💬 Think of three family members or friends. Take notes on their character. Tell your partner.

> My father's very passionate, particularly about his work.

> I really like my aunt. She's a very successful lawyer. Some people think she's arrogant, but I don't.

PRONUNCIATION *Word stress*

a ▶01.07 Listen to these adjectives and underline the stressed syllable. Which syllable is stressed: the first, second, third, or fourth?

optimistic   unsympathetic   arrogant   ambitious

b ▶01.08 Write these words in the chart. Then listen and check your answers. Practice saying the words.

passionate	self-confident	sensitive	determined
determination	pessimistic	environment	
environmental	influential	television	

1st syllable stressed	2nd syllable stressed
3rd syllable stressed	**4th syllable stressed**

c 💬 Test each other. Student A: Choose a word in **b** and say a sentence.
Student B: Did Student A say the adjective correctly?

> I'm determined to become a millionaire.

d ≫ Now go back to p. 10.

154

2A Expressions with *get*

a Read what Emma and Martin say. Who did they have a problem with?

Emma:

"Last year I decided to join the social club at work. I always thought the social club was boring, and I wanted to improve it. I talked to some other people in the club, and we tried to figure out a way to **get rid of** the man running the club – the president – because we really thought he was the problem. Everyone liked this idea, and we all **got a little carried away** and decided a direct approach would be best. At the next meeting, we were about to say something when all of a sudden he said, 'Look, I'll **get straight to the point**. I think the social club's getting too boring, and we need some fresh ideas.' We couldn't believe his sudden change. Now the club is much more interesting, lots of new people joined, and I'm glad I **got involved**."

Martin:

"My brother's really **getting on my nerves** at the moment. He won't study at all. I can't **get across** to him the importance of doing well at school. He just won't listen and it's **getting me down**. The problem is he **got through** his exams very easily last year without studying. He thinks he can do the same thing this year, but I'm not so sure."

b Match the *get* expressions in **bold** in **a** with definitions 1–8.
1 to say something important immediately and in a direct way
2 to make someone understand something
3 to take part in an activity or organization
4 to be successful in an examination or competition
5 when something annoys you
6 to become so excited about something that you are no longer careful
7 when something makes you feel sad or depressed
8 to send or throw someone or something away

c **Pronunciation** Notice the linking between *get* and the word after in this example.
I'm glad I got_involved.

▶ 02.02 Listen to these examples. In which sentences is there linking between *get* and the word after? What does that tell you about linking?
1 We tried to figure out a way to get rid of the man running the club.
2 We all got a little carried away.
3 I'll get straight to the point.
4 I can't get across to him the importance of doing well.

d Think of examples of these things.
1 a time that you got rid of something you didn't want
2 something that gets on your nerves
3 a time when you got through a presentation, test, or interview
4 a situation where you got a little carried away
5 a club or organization you got involved in

e 💬 Tell each other about your examples in **d**.

PRONUNCIATION Sound and spelling: *g*

a ▶ 02.03 Listen to the words. In which words does *g* have … ?
1 a hard sound /g/
2 a soft sound /dʒ/

get   negative   manage

b ▶ 02.04 Decide which sound the *g* has in these words – /g/ or /dʒ/. Then listen and practice saying them.

guard   gymnastics   guide   generous
biology   together   religion   agree
dangerous   forget   bridge   gardener

c Look at your answers to **b**.
1 If *g* is followed by a consonant or *a*, *o*, or *u*, is it hard or soft?
2 If *g* is followed by *e*, *i*, or *y*, is it hard or soft? Are there exceptions to this rule?

d ≫ Now go to p. 21.

3B Words connected with sports

Pablo will once again **represent** Argentina at next year's championship. He already holds the **world record** for the fastest 800m in 2018. During that race, he **led** from the beginning.

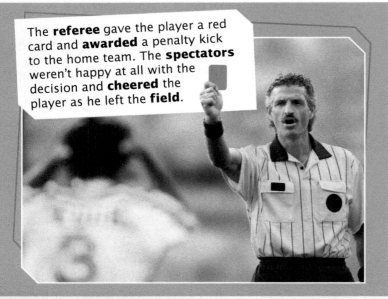

The **referee** gave the player a red card and **awarded** a penalty kick to the home team. The **spectators** weren't happy at all with the decision and **cheered** the player as he left the **field**.

a Find words in the sports reports which mean:
1 play for your country or city
2 the people watching a game
3 be ahead during a game or competition
4 give (a prize or a point) for something you have done
5 shout to show you think someone is good
6 the best or fastest that has ever been achieved
7 the person who makes decisions during a sports game
8 the area where a soccer game is played.

b Underline the correct words.
1 Even though she holds the *world record / spectator* in the 1500m, Kirabo Sanaa probably won't *represent / award* her country at the next Olympic Games.
2 The spectators *cheered / represented* as the players walked onto the *field / referee*.
3 Mateo Amador *cheered / led* the race from the beginning and was *awarded / cheered* a gold medal.

c Write two short sports reports, using two of the sentence starters. Use the words in **bold** in the texts and your own ideas.
1 Ten minutes into the game, …
2 Eighteen-year-old Maria Ortiz from Uruguay …
3 Kenyan runner Pamela Abasi …

d 💬 Read your reports aloud. Who has the most interesting sports report?

PRONUNCIATION Word stress

a Add the words in the box to the chart.

> training competition victor competitor performance championship trainer athletic competitive athletics victorious performer professional

Verb	Noun (event or activity)	Noun (person)	Adjective
compete	*competition*		
		athlete	
	victory		
		champion	
train			
perform			
	profession		professional

b ▶03.04 Which syllable is stressed in each word in the chart? Does the stress stay the same in all the word forms or does it change? Listen and check.

c ▶03.05 How does the vowel sound in **bold** change in each pair of words? Listen and check.

athl**e**te athl**e**tics
vict**o**ry vict**o**rious
comp**e**te comp**e**titor

d 💬 Work in pairs. Cover the chart and test each other.
Student A: Say a sentence with one of the words.
Student B: Make a follow-up sentence with a similar meaning, using a different word.

> He entered the championship.

> He wanted to be the champion.

e ≫ Now go back to p. 36.

4B Talking about difficulty

a <u>Underline</u> a word or phrase in each sentence that means (to be) difficult.

1 Working as a server in a busy restaurant is one of the most demanding jobs I've ever had.
2 I find it a little awkward when I have to speak to my staff about mistakes they've made.
3 Teaching a class on my own for the first time was a very testing experience.
4 Taking the outdoor survival training class really challenged me.
5 I have to talk to my teacher because I'm not happy with her lessons; it's a very challenging subject, and I'm not sure what to say exactly.
6 Unfortunately, it's often not very straightforward for students here to find part-time work.
7 When I lived in Budapest, it was a struggle to learn Hungarian well.
8 I think I understand how computers work, but learning a programming language really stretched me.

b Which word in **a** do we use to describe situations that are embarrassing or need to be dealt with very carefully?

c Complete the sentences with words in **a**. There may be more than one answer.

1 My final exams in college were really _____ / _____ – I needed a long vacation after I finished!
2 I can't go to my best friend's wedding because I'm going on vacation. It's an _____ situation, and I'm not sure how to tell her.
3 I'm really busy at work at the moment, and I'm finding it a _____ to get my work done by the end of the day.
4 I thought connecting my new printer to my computer would be easy, but actually it's not _____ at all.
5 I'm not very confident, so giving a presentation at my university last week in front of 50 people really _____ / _____ me.

d Think of an experience you've had for three of the things below.

1 an outdoor experience that stretched you
2 the most challenging thing about learning a language
3 a book you once read that wasn't straightforward
4 an awkward meeting you once had
5 a sport that was a struggle for you to learn
6 a delicate question that you had to ask someone
7 something you studied that was really tough
8 a testing experience you had in a new place or country

e 💬🗩 Now tell each other about the things you chose in **d**.

PRONUNCIATION Sound and spelling: u

a ▶ 04.07 Listen to the words.

include   struggle   cushion   busy

b Match the vowel sounds in the words in **a** with the sounds in words 1–4.

1 cup
2 put
3 true
4 thin

c ▶ 04.08 What sound does u have in these words? Listen to check and add them to the chart.

subject	focus	punish
pull	amusing	assume
unfortunately	super	pudding
business	supper	helpful

Sound 1 /ʌ/	Sound 2 /ʊ/	Sound 3 /u/ or /ju/	Sound 4 /ɪ/

d 💬🗩 Write a sentence with two of the words in **a** or **b**. Read your sentence to other students and check if you pronounced u correctly.

e ≫ Now go back to p. 49.

5A Adjectives describing attitude

a Read about Tamara's family and add adjectives in the blanks.

> thoughtful   critical   disorganized   unreliable
> well-organized   irresponsible   sympathetic   competitive

My brother Nick is very ¹_____ – his desk is a mess and he can never find anything. But my sister Vera is a very ²_____ person. She plans her day carefully, and she always knows exactly where everything is. She's also so ³_____. She wants to be the best – it's all she thinks about. I would say my grandmother is a very ⁴_____ person – you can go to her if you're in trouble and she'll always listen and make you feel better. My cousin, Maude, is very ⁵_____. She's always thinking about how she can help other people. She remembers everyone's birthday and always sends presents. I like my other cousin, Becky, but she can be pretty ⁶_____. She never tells anyone where she's going when she goes out, and she sometimes leaves the front door open or doesn't lock her car. She's also terribly ⁷_____. If you arrange to meet her somewhere, she'll probably be late or she won't even show up. And what about me? Everyone in the family complains that I'm always commenting on what people are like. Some of them say I'm too ⁸_____ and I only see the bad things in them. I can't imagine why they would think that.

b Complete the chart. Use prefixes or suffixes to make the opposites of the adjectives in **a**.

thoughtful	
well-organized	disorganized
	unreliable
	irresponsible
sympathetic	
competitive	
critical	

c Make a list of the prefixes and suffixes we can add to adjectives to make them negative.

d ▶ 05.01 Look at the sentences. Decide if the word in **bold** is correct or not. Then listen and check.
1 He often arrives late to meetings and doesn't bring everything he needs. He's very **disorganized**.
2 She always makes sensible decisions, and she never does anything silly. She's very **irresponsible**.
3 She often expresses negative opinions about things and other people. She's very **critical**.
4 If he says he's going to do something, he always does it. He's very **reliable**.
5 He doesn't think about how the things he says might affect other people. He's totally **thoughtful**.
6 When you tell her your problems, she listens and tries to understand how you feel. She's **unsympathetic**.
7 He always wants to do better than everyone else. He's very **competitive**.

e Look through the adjectives and their opposites and write down your own personality "profile."

f 💬 Tell your partner and mention a few examples of things you do.

> I think I'm fairly thoughtful and caring. For example, I call my grandmother once a week to ask how she is …

PRONUNCIATION   Sound and spelling: *th*

a ▶ 05.02 Listen to *th* in these words. What two different sounds do you hear?

thoughtful	clothes
weather	seventh
sympathetic	

b ▶ 05.03 Which sound does *th* have in these words? Listen to check, then add them to the chart.

leather	north
thumb	northern
month	Netherlands
together	healthy
something	enthusiastic
therefore	worth

Sound 1 /θ/ (think)	Sound 2 /ð/ (the)

c ≫ Now go to p. 58.

This page is intentionally left blank.

Phonemic symbols

Vowel sounds

/ə/	/æ/	/ʊ/	/ɑ/	/ɜ/	/u/	/ɔ/
teach**er**	m**a**n	p**u**t	g**o**t	sh**ir**t	wh**o**	w**a**lk

/ɪ/	/i/	/e/	/ʌ/			
ch**i**p	happ**y**	m**e**n	b**u**t			

Diphthongs (two vowel sounds)

/eə/	/ɪə/	/ɔɪ/	/ɑɪ/	/eɪ/	/oʊ/	/aʊ/
h**air**	n**ear**	b**oy**	f**i**ne	l**a**te	c**oa**t	n**ow**

Consonants

/p/	/b/	/f/	/v/	/t/	/d/	/k/	/g/	/θ/	/ð/	/tʃ/	/dʒ/
pill	**b**ook	**f**ace	**v**an	**t**ime	**d**og	**c**old	**g**o	**th**irty	**th**ey	**ch**oose	**j**eans

/s/	/z/	/ʃ/	/ʒ/	/m/	/n/	/ŋ/	/h/	/l/	/r/	/w/	/j/
say	**z**ero	**sh**oe	u**s**ually	**m**e	**n**ow	si**ng**	**h**ot	**l**ate	**r**ed	**w**ent	**y**es

Irregular verbs

Infinitive	Simple past	Past participle
be	was / were	been
become	became	become
blow	blew	blown
break	broke	broken
bring	brought	brought
build	built	built
buy	bought	bought
catch	caught	caught
choose	chose	chosen
come	came	come
cost	cost	cost
cut	cut	cut
deal	dealt	dealt
do	did	done
draw	drew	drawn
drink	drank	drunk
drive	drove	driven
eat	ate	eaten
fall	fell	fallen
feel	felt	felt
find	found	found
fly	flew	flown
forget	forgot	forgotten
get	got	gotten
give	gave	given
go	went	gone
grow	grew	grown
have	had	had
hear	heard	heard
hide	hid	hidden
hit	hit	hit
hold	held	held
keep	kept	kept
know	knew	known
lead	led	led

Infinitive	Simple past	Past participle
learn	learned	learned
leave	left	left
lend	lent	lent
let	let	let
lose	lost	lost
make	made	made
meet	met	met
pay	paid	paid
put	put	put
read	read	read
ride	rode	ridden
ring	rang	rung
run	ran	run
sink	sank	sunk
say	said	said
see	saw	seen
sell	sold	sold
set	set	set
sing	sang	sung
sleep	slept	slept
speak	spoke	spoken
spend	spent	spent
stand	stood	stood
steal	stole	stolen
swim	swam	swum
take	took	taken
teach	taught	taught
tell	told	told
think	thought	thought
throw	threw	thrown
understand	understood	understood
wake	woke	woken
wear	wore	worn
win	won	won
write	wrote	written

Acknowledgments

The authors and publishers acknowledge the following sources of copyright material and are grateful for the permissions granted. While every effort has been made, it has not always been possible to identify the sources of all the material used, or to trace all copyright holders. If any omissions are brought to our notice, we will be happy to include the appropriate acknowledgements on reprinting and in the next update to the digital edition, as applicable.

Key:
U = Unit, C = Communication, V = Vocabulary.

Text
U2: The New Zealand Herald for the extract from 'Robert Hewitt's story of survival', by Leah Haines, *The New Zealand Herald, 19/03/2006.* Reproduced with permission; **C**: Extract from 'Separated twin boys with almost identical lives', *Reader's Digest.* Copyright 1980 Reader's Digest magazine. Reproduced with kind permission.

Photography
All the photographs are sourced from Getty Images.
U1: Ullstein bild; Taylor Hill/FilmMagic; Justin Sullivan/Staff/ Getty Images News; Patrick McMullan; De Agostini/Icas94/De Agostini Picture Library/Getty Images Plus; Daily Herald Archive/ SSPL; Handout/Getty Images News; Thomas Barwick/DigitalVision; Westend61; PixelsEffect/E+; Tim Robberts/Stone; Tim Robberts/ DigitalVision; FG Trade/E+; GlobalStock/E+; Aldomurillo/E+; Maridav/ iStock/Getty Images Plus; Maskot; Filadendron/E+; Lilly Roadstones/ Stone; **U2:** JUSTIN TALLIS/AFP; Jeff Rotman/Photolibrary/Getty Images Plus; Zac Macaulay/The Image Bank/Getty Images Plus; Frederic Pacorel/Photolibrary/Getty Images Plus; Jenny & Tony Enderby/Lonely Planet Images/Getty Images Plus; Bingokid/E+; Vav63/ iStock/Getty Images Plus; Lori Adamski Peek/Photolibrary/Getty Images Plus; Martin Harvey/DigitalVision; ePhotocorp/iStock/Getty Images Plus; Zdenek Maly/EyeEm; Maxime Riendeau/500px Prime; Martin Mecnarowski/500Px Plus; Andy2673/iStock/Getty Images Plus; Ma-no/iStock/Getty Images Plus; Chris Jongkind/Moment; Dhsueh/ iStock/Getty Images Plus; Paddy Eckersley/Photodisc; Christopher Pillitz/Hulton Archive; ULTRA.F/The Image Bank/Getty Images Plus; Tetra Images; Witold Skrypczak/Lonely Planet Images/Getty Images Plus; Marco Livolsi/EyeEm; Yasuhide Fumoto/Photodisc; **U3:** Thomas_EyeDesign/E+; Hill Street Studios/DigitalVision; Luis Alvarez/DigitalVision; Kimberrywood/iStock/Getty Images Plus; Drbouz/ E+; Cecilie_Arcurs/E+; Kasto80/iStock/Getty Images Plus; Vgajic/E+; Paul Kane/Stringer/Getty Images Sport; Laurence Griffiths/Staff/Getty Images Sport; Tim Clayton/Corbis Sport; STAFF/AFP; John Dorton/ ISI Photos/Getty Images Sport; OLAF KRAAK/Staff/AFP; PhotoAlto/ Sandro Di Carlo Darsa/PhotoAlto Agency RF Collections; Michael Steele/Staff/Getty Images Sport; Tim de Waele/Staff/Velo; VCG/Visual China Group; Matt Sullivan/Stringer/Getty Images Sport; Westend61; Vladimir Godnik; Sportstock/E+; FatCamera/E+; Thomas Barwick/ DigitalVision; **U4:** Marko Geber/DigitalVision; GlobalStock/E+; Laboko/ iStock/Getty Images Plus; Ariel Skelley/DigitalVision; Andresr/E+; Ty Downing/Photolibrary/Getty Images Plus/; FG Trade/E+; Fairfax Media; Education Images/Universal Images Group; Extreme-photographer/iStock/Getty Images Plus; Ade_Deployed/E+; Sam Edwards/OJO Images; Jay Yuno/E+; Stephen Dorey/The Image Bank/ Getty Images Plus; Travelpix Ltd/Stone; Tadamasa Taniguchi/Stone; Sisoje/E+; Mariusz_prusaczyk/iStock Editorial/Getty Images Plus; Tuul & Bruno Morandi/The Image Bank; FG Trade/E+; Westend61; Morsa Images/E+; Michaeljung/iStock/Getty Images Plus; **U5:** Frans Lemmens/The Image Bank Unreleased; Hinterhaus Productions/ DigitalVision; Meredith Heil/iStock/Getty Images Plus; Charlie Waite/ The Image Bank/Getty Images Plus; JohnnyGreig/E+; Brett Phibbs/ Image Source; DigitalGlobe/ScapeWare3d/DigitalGlobe; Paul Souders/ Stone; Joseph Van Os/The Image Bank/Getty Images Plus; Andresr/ E+; William King/Taxi/Getty Images Plus; Juanmonino/E+; Chasing Light - Photography by James Stone james-stone.com/Moment; Simon Bottomley/DigitalVision; Ales-A/E+; Jamie Grill; Spondylolithesis/iStock Unreleased; Richard Clark/The Image Bank; Andrew Merry/Moment; Jens Kuhfs/The Image Bank/Getty Images Plus; Damir Khabirov/ iStock/Getty Images Plus.

Cover photography by cdbrphotography/iStock/Getty Images Plus/Getty Images.

Illustration
QBS Learning; David Semple; Dusan Lakicevic; Gavin Reece; Jerome Mireault; Jo Goodberry; John (KJA Artists); Marie-Eve Tremblay; Mark Bird; Mark Duffin; Martin Sanders; Paul Williams; Roger Penwill; Sean (KJA Artists); Sean Sims.

Audio Production by John Marshall Media.

Corpus
Development of this publication has made use of the Cambridge English Corpus(CEC). The CEC is a computer database of contemporary spoken and written English, which currently stands at over one billion words. It includes British English, American English and other varieties of English. It also includes the Cambridge Learner Corpus, developed in collaboration with the University of Cambridge ESOL Examinations. Cambridge University Press has built up the CEC to provide evidence about language use that helps us to produce better language teaching materials.

English Profile
This product is informed by English Vocabulary Profile, built as part of English Profile, a collaborative program designed to enhance the learning, teaching and assessment of English worldwide. Its main funding partners are Cambridge University Press and Cambridge Assessment English and its aim is to create a "profile" for English, linked to the Common European Framework of Reference for Languages (CEFR). English Profile outcomes, such as the English Vocabulary Profile, will provide detailed information about the language that learners can be expected to demonstrate at each CEFR level, offering a clear benchmark for learners' proficiency. For more information, please visit www.englishprofile.org.

CALD
The Cambridge Advanced Learner's Dictionary is the world's most widely used dictionary for learners of English. Including all the words and phrases that learners are likely to come across, it also has easy-to-understand definitions and example sentences to show how the word is used in context. The Cambridge Advanced Learner's Dictionary is available online at dictionary.cambridge.org.

Shaftesbury Road, Cambridge CB2 8EA, United Kingdom

One Liberty Plaza, 20th Floor, New York, NY 10006, USA

477 Williamstown Road, Port Melbourne, VIC 3207, Australia

314–321, 3rd Floor, Plot 3, Splendor Forum, Jasola District Centre, New Delhi – 110025, India

103 Penang Road, #05–06/07, Visioncrest Commercial, Singapore 238467

Cambridge University Press & Assessment is a department of the University of Cambridge.

We share the University's mission to contribute to society through the pursuit of education, learning and research at the highest international levels of excellence.

www.cambridge.org
Information on this title: www.cambridge.org/9781108861427

First published 2022

20 19 18 17 16 15 14 13 12 11 10 9 8 7 6 5 4 3 2

Printed in Great Britain by CPI Group (UK) Ltd, Croydon CR0 4YY

A catalogue record for this publication is available from the British Library

ISBN 978-1-108-81719-6 Upper Intermediate Student's Book with eBook
ISBN 978-1-108-81730-1 Upper Intermediate Student's Book A with eBook
ISBN 978-1-108-81731-8 Upper Intermediate Student's Book B with eBook
ISBN 978-1-108-86138-0 Upper Intermediate Student's Book with Digital Pack
ISBN 978-1-108-86142-7 Upper Intermediate Student's Book A with Digital Pack
ISBN 978-1-108-86143-4 Upper Intermediate Student's Book B with Digital Pack
ISBN 978-1-108-81720-2 Upper Intermediate Workbook with Answers
ISBN 978-1-108-81722-6 Upper Intermediate Workbook A with Answers
ISBN 978-1-108-81723-3 Upper Intermediate Workbook B with Answers
ISBN 978-1-108-81724-0 Upper Intermediate Workbook without Answers
ISBN 978-1-108-81725-7 Upper Intermediate Workbook A without Answers
ISBN 978-1-108-81726-4 Upper Intermediate Workbook B without Answers
ISBN 978-1-108-81727-1 Upper Intermediate Full Contact with eBook
ISBN 978-1-108-81728-8 Upper Intermediate Full Contact A with eBook
ISBN 978-1-108-81729-5 Upper Intermediate Full Contact B with eBook
ISBN 978-1-108-86139-7 Upper Intermediate Full Contact with Digital Pack
ISBN 978-1-108-86140-3 Upper Intermediate Full Contact A with Digital Pack
ISBN 978-1-108-86141-0 Upper Intermediate Full Contact B with Digital Pack
ISBN 978-1-108-81732-5 Upper Intermediate Teacher's Book with Digital Pack
ISBN 978-1-108-81717-2 Upper Intermediate Presentation Plus

Additional resources for this publication at www.cambridge.org/americanempower

Cambridge University Press & Assessment has no responsibility for the persistence or accuracy of URLs for external or third-party internet websites referred to in this publication, and does not guarantee that any content on such websites is, or will remain, accurate or appropriate. Information regarding prices, travel timetables, and other factual information given in this work is correct at the time of first printing but Cambridge University Press & Assessment does not guarantee the accuracy of such information thereafter.

This page is intentionally left blank.

This page is intentionally left blank.